Aztecs
& Maya

Aztecs
& Maya

N. James

First published 2001, reprinted 2005. This edition 2009

The History Press
The Mill, Brimscombe Port
Stroud, Gloucestershire, GL5 2QG
www.thehistorypress.co.uk

British Library Cataloguing in Publication Data.
A catalogue record for this book is available from the British Library.

ISBN 978 0 7524 5428 3

Typesetting and origination by The History Press
Printed in Great Britain

Contents

Acknowledgements

Plates 1 and 32 are the work of Julie Coimbra. Of the others: plate 14 is reproduced by courtesy of the Cambridge University Museum of Archaeology & Anthropology; 16 (and the back cover image) was kindly contributed by David and Emma Parkin; and 30 is from R. Gallop *Mexican Mosaic* (1939 London: Faber). Fig 4 is from T.U. Brocklehurst *Mexico today* (1883 London: John Murray); fig 18 is from T. Proskouriakoff (1946 *An album of Maya architecture* Washington DC: Carnegie Institution); fig 22, by Frederick Catherwood, is from J.L. Stephens *Incidents of travel in Central America, Chiapas and Yucatan* (1841 New York: Harper); figs 26, 28, 30 and 33 are adapted from A. Aglio *Antiquities of Mexico* (Vol I 1830 London: Viscount Kingsborough); and fig 38 is from F. del Paso *Papeles de Nueva España* (1905 2nd ser. Vol 6 Madrid: Suc. de Rivadeneyra). Figures 26, 28, 30 and 33 are reproduced by permission of the Syndics of Cambridge University Library.

Pronunciation and spelling

It all comes right with practice! In Nahuatl, the stress normally falls on the penultimate syllable but, in Maya languages, on the last. In this book, exceptions are accented as in Spanish, e.g. Tehuacán (Teotihuacan is often pronounced this way too), and the same is done for other languages, such as Purépecha.

'X' represents a range from 'h' in Oaxaca to 'sh' in Mexica or Yaxchilan to a soft 'z' in Xochicalco. Nahuatl final -tl is silent, so Nahuatl is pronounced 'Nahuat'.

For Maya languages, the new convention on spelling is used here except for very common names like Yucatan. There is not yet consensus on all of these spellings. In words like Tik'al, the ' is a glottal stop like 'the tt in ... Cockney ... bottle', as Prof. Coe explains in *The Maya* p.9 (see References, for chapter 1).

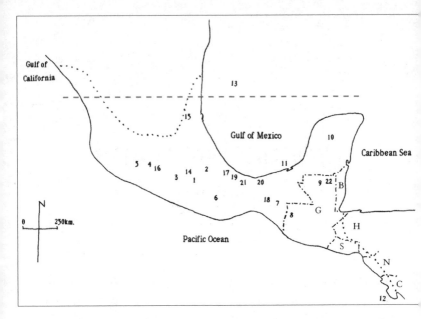

1 Mesoamerica: 1 Morelos; 2 Puebla Basin; 3 Toluca Basin; 4 Michoacán basins;
5 Chapala Basin; 6 Valley of Oaxaca; 7 Chiapas; 8 Maya highlands; 9 Peten;
10 Yucatan; 11 Lago de Términos; 12 Nicoya Peninsula; 13 Tropic of Cancer;
14 Tenochtitlan, Coapexco Teotihuacan (Valley of Mexico); 15 Tantoc
16 Tzintzuntzan; 17 La Mojarra; 18 Chiapa de Corzo; 19 Tres Zapotes; 20 San
Andrés; 21 San Lorenzo Tenochtitlán; 22 San Bartolo. The dotted lines mark the
area's maximum pre-Spanish extent; dot-&-dash lines mark today's international
frontiers pre-Spanish extent. Dot-&-dash lines mark today's international
frontiers east of Mexico: B Belize; G Guatemala; H Honduras; S El Salvador; N
Nicaragua; C Costa Rica

1

The middle world

The country of the Aztecs, the Maya and the other Native peoples of tropical Mexico and western Central America is known as Mesoamerica (*1*). It is a 'culture area', defined not by physical geography but by a way of life. In the east live the Maya, in the western part have lived the Aztecs and many other peoples less famous but whose histories also figure in this book.

Mesoamericans are Indians (plate 1). Along with the great majority of the other Native peoples of the Americas, they share a distinct biological heritage. New research is complicating the story, but it is unlikely to change the principle that all of them are descended from small populations of Siberian colonists arriving through North America roughly 20,000 years ago.

By the time of the Spanish Conquest, nearly 500 years ago, there were about 25 million people in Mesoamerica. It was the most populous area in the Americas; and it had probably been so for 3000 years. The greater proportion lived in the west, although, today, the Maya amount to more than half of the roughly 15 million Mesoamericans.

LANGUAGE

Mexican sociologists and anthropologists commonly regard language as a mark of ethnic identity. While Mesoamericans have more in common with each other than with other Indians to the north and south, great linguistic variety matches other evidence for a long and complicated history (*2*).

The languages of the west are especially diverse. The Aztecs' was Nahuatl, one of a group of languages spoken in several different regions and related to others as far north as Utah. That distribution suggests a long history of colonization but there is doubt as to whether early farmers in Central Mexico were the original speakers or whether these languages were late introduced from the north. Other evidence tends to confirm that there were migrations; but it is more or less guesswork as to what languages were spoken in particular places before AD 1000 as witness, for example, current debate about the origin and early distribution of the word 'cacao' (for chocolate).

There are more than two dozen Maya languages. Except for Huastec, in the north, the distribution suggests that the Maya are long rooted in the east. Yet, despite a great number of written texts of the first millennium AD, it is not known for sure what language most Maya spoke in that era of glories, partly because their writing did not correspond wholly to speech and partly because all their inscriptions may have favoured a single formal language (3).

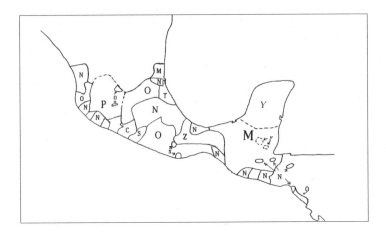

2 Languages: approximate distribution of main groups in the sixteenth century. C Cuitlatec; M Maya; N Uto-Nahua/Aztecan (including Cora and Huichol in the west and Pipil in Central America); O Oto-Mangueyan (including Zapotec, Mixtec, Matlazinca and Mazahua); P Purépecha; S Tlapanec & Tequistlatec; T Totonac & Tepehua; Y Yucatec Maya; Z Mixe-Zoquean

The best bets are that they spoke forms of Chol in the populous central region (still spoken in the western part), and almost certainly Yucatec in the north.

Some languages are historically anomalous. The principal puzzle is Purépecha, the language of the Aztecs' rivals, the Tarascans. Some scholars detect links far to the north, others to South America and others align it with the Maya languages.

BALANCING THE WORLD

Linguistic diversity notwithstanding, the chief feature that distinguishes Mesoamerica past and present is a common core of ideas. Every community has the concept of its own central place or 'navel'. Each of the cardinal directions is associated with certain colours, certain moral qualities and certain spirits; and there is the concept of a vertical dimension, through the centre, from heaven, in which Mesoamericans used to distinguish nine levels or 13, to the underworld, in which they distinguished nine; there is some

3 Maya glyphic writing: upper left, 'Lord of Mutal' (Tik'al); upper right, 'Lord of Palenque'; lower left, Bird Jaguar (royal name at Yaxchilan); lower right, Thirteen Muan (a calendric spirit)

evidence for these distinctions in contemporary symbolism too. The centre, commonly a spring or a hill, is marked, as a shrine, by a pyramid or, since the Spanish Conquest, a cross. The concept is of an island or a mountain which, connected with the spirits of the world, is a source of life. The same idea holds good at different scales from household to village to nation.

The Mesoamerican world is governed by spirits (4). The fate of communities and of every person depends on them. So harmony with the spirits is literally vital. Shrines and temples or churches were and are the principal places for ensuring it. At the time of the Spanish Conquest, one of the most critical rites was the Ball Game, in which teams competed with a rubber ball along a court in the form of the letter I. For the Aztecs, the ball represented the Sun and the court the underworld: the Game was a means for people, in their middle plane, to assess the cosmos. Usually, the losers were given the honour of sacrifice to 'the gods'. Yet, it was thought – and it still is – that fate can be influenced by aligning people with the spirits, by proper behaviour. Equally, of course, bad conduct invites bad consequences.

The concept of soul is consistent with these ideas. Balance among the hot and the cold energies flowing through the world was axiomatic in Aztec medicine. By the same token, the soul was and is commonly thought to comprise one part within the body and another outside. Maintenance of this complicated harmony is one of the skills of curers or shamans.

Dependence on the spirits that govern the world is expressed in the Aztec myth of origin. The best known version, the Legend of the Suns, described four previous worlds and then the agonies that the gods endured in order to create the present one: first, one had to burn himself to make the Sun; then Quetzalcoatl, the Feathered Serpent, hazarded himself down among the dead to collect bones for creating people; with his own blood, he gave them life; and then the gods had to undertake further sacrifices to maintain life by giving the Sun movement. Most beautiful of the myths is the Popol Vuh, 'Genesis' of the K'iche' Maya, which describes the stillness before the gods separated earth from ocean, and explains how they created people to acknowledge them with sacrifices of their own and with prayer.

One of the key symbols for Mesoamericans is time. Intellectuals considered that it is important to observe how bad periods follow auspicious times and are succeeded, in turn, by better periods. Some rural communities still observe the process. They use three principles. First, time is considered to spiral: 'no given time', discovered Barbara Tedlock, 'can be totally isolated from the segments of time that precede or follow'. Second, two main cycles run simultaneously: the solar year, calculated as 365 days, and a sacred round of 260 days. Third, just as days pass within years and years within centuries, Mesoamerican time has concentric dimensions.

The sacred round is peculiar to Mesoamerica. Various attempts have been made to explain it. Comprising 13 cycles of 20 named days, it related to the solar year on the principle that it takes 52 years to realize every combination of each day in the respective rounds. A welter of numerological implications spin out from this formula. Aztecs and others named children for the ritual dates of their birth.

Since it comprises several cycles, observation and interpretation of time could be difficult. Astronomers recorded both the common regularities – such as the Sun's course across the sky and along the horizons, or the phases of the Moon – and occurrences such as comets, which, though rare, were not regarded as chance events. The combined cycle of the solar and sacred years was related to that of Venus: every other time that the 52 year round is completed, Venus completes 65 cycles across the sky. The Maya, especially, took such calculations to great lengths. The thirteenth-century Dresden Codex, for instance – one of only three or four known Maya books (or parts of books) to survive the Spanish Conquest in legible condition – comprises almanacs, tables for relating eclipses to the movement of Venus, and prophecies.

In the first millennium AD, the Maya dated royal events in relation to a Long Count. Deriving it from calculations with the numbers 20 and 13, they fixed its start at 3114 BC and expected it to end in AD 2012. For certain purposes, they dated events to much longer cycles. Described by arithmetic and verified by astronomy, time's cycles are still interpreted, in some communities, by the higher art of astrology, as the operation of everything that happens.

4 Coatlicue, 'Snake Skirt', Aztec earth spirit. Basalt, she stands 3.5m high. Now exhibited in the National Museum of Anthropology, Mexico City

Accordingly, rites, periodical and occasional, provide a framework for proper witness.

Mesoamericans tend to think of the world as an organization of complementary pairs (*34*): the parts of the soul, for example, heat and cold, outside and inside, east and west, Sun and Moon, war and peace – most basically, the living and the dead. Was it this concept that gave rise to settlements laid out in paired parts, from Coapexco, more than 3000 years ago, to some Aztec villages and even their capital, and to a few villages right down to today? Anthropologists have long debated the proposition that ideas spring from social organisation; but for one thing, not all such villages today do arrange daily life around the division; and, for another, there is an argument that dualism is a principle brought in by the Spaniards. More broadly, E.Z.Vogt has discovered that Maya 'replicate' their 'model . . . of the natural and cultural world . . . at each level of . . . society and . . . in different domains of . . . culture', while James Lockhart finds that, in the early Colonial period, the Aztecs recognized 'unity . . . in the symmetrical numerical arrangement of . . . parts, their identical relationship to a common . . . point, and their orderly, cyclical rotation' – a 'cellular or modular' principle (see References). Not that Mesoamericans put it like this: their thought is characteristically applied, not theoretical. While their reformed or 'born again' Christian neighbours talk of themselves as what they *are*, reports R.S. Carlsen, traditional Tz'utujil Maya call themselves Working People who 'perform rituals to help move the sun'.

Social anthropologists and sociologists have long wondered about connections between thought and social organization. In Mesoamerica today, links can be found where households share work on each other's fields or in communal projects, when house-holders complement each other by sharing contributions in village rites and feasts or, most basically, when they exchange partners in marriage. In ancient times, ceremonies among the pyramids and ball courts may have tended to 'centre' people on more public symbols; but does the underlying sense of local identity help to explain Mesoamerica's endurance?

ABUNDANCE, DIVERSITY AND DANGER

Of all their vivid colours, ancient Mesoamericans loved best the greens and turquoise of quetzal plumes and jadeite or 'greenstone' for their suggestions of lush crops. Yet, sensitive to tragedy for so many reasons, the Indians are not just cheery optimists. The climate itself encourages a dualistic outlook: from September (or now October) to May (or now June), it is generally dry and bright, but from May or June to October (and later in the east) rains beat in from the east.

The landscape is very diverse, moreover, and symbolism varies accordingly. Where the Earth Lord is emphasized in the tumultu-ous mountains, it is weather spirits in Yucatan, where the hazards are drought and hurricanes (9). Diversity, in turn, may have bred alertness to complementarity. W.T. Sanders and others have argued that much of Mesoamerica's history, up to the Spanish Conquest, depended on 'symbiotic' exchanges between environments. These ecological relations tended to set Mesoamerica apart from neigh-bouring regions (1). Time and again, for example, archaeology shows connections along the isthmus between the Gulf of Mexico, to the northwest, and southernmost Mexico; and the distribution of Maya languages shows the same pattern (*2*).

At the time of the Conquest, Central Mexico was the most populous region. Like its successor, Mexico City, today, and Teotihuacan long before, Tenochtitlan, the Aztec capital, was one of the world's half dozen largest cities. It was surrounded by scores of other towns and hundreds of villages. Tzintzuntzan, the Tarascan capital, had about 30,000 inhabitants and was also surrounded by scores of villages. The Maya, in the east, lived in villages around modest towns in Yucatan and the southern highlands, but although populous six centuries before, northern Guatemala and southern Yucatan were now thinly peopled.

The great majority of people throughout have lived by subsistence farming. Most of the country is prodigiously fertile. The main foods were – and are – maize, beans and squash, while cotton and maguey (agave or century plant, related to aloe) were grown for textiles. Little meat was eaten, since, until the Spanish Conquest, there were no domesticable herd animals. Hence too, human brawn was the only source of power.

Western Mesoamerica is dominated by two ranges of mountains with a series of basins between them, the Basin or Valley of Mexico, hearth of the Aztecs, the Puebla basin, to the east, and others to the west, including the heartland of the Tarascans. The Basin of Mexico and the western basins have – or had – large lakes. Volcanic eruptions and earthquakes are common. To the north, the basins give way to broad plains stretching, progressively drier, all the way to Arizona and New Mexico.

The Maya inhabit four landscapes. In the south, a hot plain shelves from the ocean to the mountains, which are almost as high as Central Mexico's and just as prone to earthquakes and eruptions. Northward, in turn, lies the central region, low country (now under the worldwide assault on rainforest); and then Yucatan, where the vegetation grows progressively sparser and lower to the north. Easier travel across much of eastern Mesoamerica may help to explain how language and other cultural traits were more widely shared than in the west (*2*).

Geographers of Mesoamerica use Spanish phrases to distinguish three kinds of country, tierra, by altitude. Up to 1km above sea level lies tierra caliente, hot country, including a broad, humid coastal plain along the Gulf of Mexico. Between about 1 and 2km above sea level is tierra templada, temperate, with a Mediterranean climate. Above about 2km it is 'cold', tierra fría, with the risk, in Central Mexico, of night frost over three months. There lived the Aztecs and Tarascans.

Mesoamerica's boundaries have fluctuated in response to both climate and political factors. Its maximum extent was about 500 years before the Spanish Conquest. Some archaeologists discern its influence well to the north at that time too; and, in effect, the Spanish tried to push the boundary northward in the late sixteenth century with Indian colonists from Central Mexico.

THE PATTERN OF HISTORY

Mesoamerica's characteristics – villages and towns, farming, symbolism – did not coalesce until the second millennium BC. Yet, in order to understand the history, it is necessary to know how those features developed before then as well as since. Figure 5 sets out a framework of phases. The terminology is a convention, not necessarily describing the character of life in one period and another.

The single most important point to grasp about all native traditions in the Americas is that, once the erstwhile Siberians had arrived, there was hardly any contact with the Old World until Columbus's landfall in 1492. Some scholars, comparing the separate social and political histories of the Old World – Mesopotamia, northern China and other ancient hearths of civilization – with the Americas up to 1500, have discerned broad similarities and deduced that human social organization undergoes an inevitable evolution. More important, from the indigenous point of view, is that isolation made the Americas fatally susceptible to the new colonists from the 1490s onward.

There are claims that people reached Mexico by 20,000 BC but the earliest direct evidence that all archaeologists accept is from about 10,000 BC, the Paleoindian period. With fitfully but progressively warming climate – a worldwide development following the 'Ice Age' – began the long Archaic period, in

DATE	PHASE	SUBPHASE
	Republican	
1822	Colonial	
1650		Early
1521	Postclassic	Late
1200		
900	Classic	Epiclassic
600		Late
200 AD BC 400	Formative	Late Middle
1000		Early
2000	Archaic	
3000	Paleoindian	

5 Historical periods, distinguishing pertinent subphases

about 8000 BC. The Archaic was distinguished by three mutually reinforcing processes: diminishing mobility, as people gradually settled longer in single places; rising population; and adoption of gardening and farming instead of gathering and hunting. These developments are covered in the next chapter.

Permanent villages and farming were established during the earlier second millennium BC. Archaeologists recognize this as the beginning of the Formative or Preclassic period. A critical question is whether earlier households or local 'segments' of society enjoyed greater autonomy than later and, if so, how this 'level of . . . society' was eventually subsumed. To think about this in the following chapters, it will be helpful to ask how households grew their food, or later, bought it, how they related to other households in the same village or elsewhere in work, ceremonies and marriage; and then how both farms and villages related to the environment, physical, social, political and perhaps, spiritual. With rising population, land becomes an increasingly critical resource.

The Formative stretches up to the third century AD but, by then, a second transformation had taken place in some regions, the development of the state. This transformation took as much as 1000 years, into the Classic period.

As in other parts of the world, the state arose in response to the social and political opportunities and problems of village life. They had been solved, in the first place, by chieftains; but, based on a clearer distinction between rulers and subjects, states more effectively designed and implemented policies for large populations. Some archaeologists assume that they were built on consensus, others that it was a process of extortion. Again, though, the question is as to how chiefdoms were united or transformed: there are hints of ambivalence about political power in Olmec sculptures of 1000 BC (plate 5) and among the Maya and Aztecs even much later; and, compared to the earlier phases of the Formative period, rapid successions of monuments and art styles show that, other, perhaps, than Teotihuacan (plate 9), the larger chiefdoms and the states were unstable.

Whose were those symbols, then? Were they widely accepted or merely the ideology of a remoter aristocracy? Were they addressed to local followers or more to rival nobles? By what means, economic as well as political and ritual, did communities cohere? Despite much archaeological research, little is known of how the first states worked. It is partly because, unlike research on earlier stages of the Formative, insufficient attention has been devoted to the everyday life of villages and fields. To be sure, this 'level of society' changed little from Formative times to the Spanish

period: the social organization, politics and economics of villages
remained viable, and some of the reversals in the towns were probably inflicted, like the Maya rebellions of the Modern period, by
disillusioned villagers. The development of villages, chiefdoms and
states is covered in chapters 3, 4 and 5.

The grandest chiefdoms and early states were succeeded by smaller
ones. That probably reveals the limit to which 'cellular' or 'mechanical'
organization could be extended; and also the development of institutions through which more people could depend on each other for
technical, ritual and political functions than in earlier Formative villages.
R.E. Blanton and colleagues have inferred that complex integration
was achieved, in one period or region and another, either by distribut-
ing power among various institutions – a 'corporate' strategy – or, to
the contrary, by concentrating power in monarchs and promoting their
claims with other communities or their leaders – a 'network' strategy.

Thanks, in large part, to progress in decipherment of Maya writing
and great investment in archaeological digs by the Mexican government during the 1990s, it is now clear that the seventh and eighth
centuries AD were a period of marvellous creativity among the royal
courts; but, again, without more research on how they articulated with
village life, neither the period itself nor its aftermath can be understood. Can we work out which was more critical, the institutions of
the state or the demands of urbanism? The 'collapse' of the Classic
period Maya cities, in particular, remains one of the world's great
archaeological mysteries. Many scholars blame a shift of climate so
it is interesting that, where M.D. Coe once pointed to similarities
between the Maya and the medieval Khmer in Cambodia, there is
now evidence for attributing the ruin of Angkor Wat to drought. Or
was it more a political crisis? But for local economies that preserved
some autonomy from the royal courts, could states of the Classic
period have reformed themselves to survive such challenges?

The legendary Toltecs of the eleventh and twelfth centuries are
commonly credited with the restoration of Mesoamerican civilization; but, in the light of the new discoveries, their supposed importance will be played down in this book. The later first millennium
and the first centuries of the second are covered in chapters 5 and 6.

In the fourteenth century, new powers began to emerge. Pre-

eminent were the Aztecs, their spectacular – notorious – rites reflecting or even forging their social and cultural history. That is the subject
of chapter 7. The Aztecs are doubly important because so much more
is known about them than about their ancestors that they may offer
tests for general questions about prehispanic (pre-Spanish) history.

The last two chapters bring the story up to today. Following
the Spanish Conquest of the Aztecs in 1521, Mesoamerica was
quickly ruined. By 1650, there was little reason to expect that the
tradition would survive. Unlike most of the New Englanders, the
Spanish did not want to lose the natives of their 'new world'; but
they had little more control over the basic cause of disaster than
the Indians themselves. It was biology: during the millennia of
separation between the Americas and the Old World, diseases had
developed, among Asians, Europeans and Africans, to which the
populations of the Americas had no immunity. That any of the
peoples of Mesoamerica survived, that Mesoamerica still exists, was
by dint of the Indians' own social, religious, linguistic, technological
and political strategies, and by virtue of the durability of village life.
With similar feats elsewhere in the Americas, their survival is one
of world history's epics. However, by directing labour and seizing
the land, the Europeans did weaken the villages' stability.

It is perhaps appropriate that the most famous features of
Mesoamerican history are the prehispanic pyramids and human
sacrifice. They were built or perpetrated at ever larger scales as
populations grew; and, as societies fragmented, so these gestures
diminished. Historical imagination varied by the same token, stag-
geringly broad among aristocrats at the climax of Maya civilization but parochial during the embattled Colonial period. Time,
sacrifice and sacred places have always remained cardinal symbols.
Archaeology and history reveal them at various levels of society;
but, primarily, they spring from the requirements and experiences
of the village.

WHAT KIND OF HISTORY?

What makes for a convincing, satisfying or fair account of history? It depends on judgements about three principles: how things

happen; forms of evidence; and who or what the evidence reveals
– who or what is to be studied.

For the historian, the simplest way to explain change is to ascribe
it to things impinging from outside. Climate, for example, was one
condition for rising populations about 9000 years ago in Mexico, as
in other parts of the world. Local events too could be catalytic: the
volcanic eruption which destroyed its rival almost certainly helped
to stimulate development at Teotihuacan; and it has been suggested
that another eruption contributed to the city's decline and that of
Cholula too, in the Puebla basin. Population growth too is sometimes
analysed as a challenge to social and political organization. Again,
many archaeologists, like Prof. Sanders, explain development as the
effect of economic complements between communities in different
environments – hence, they argue, interference in temperate Morelos
from the adjacent high country by both Teotihuacan and, a thousand
years later, the Aztecs.

Some archaeologists have tried to attribute features of
Mesoamerican culture to other peoples. There is evidence for
influence from South America; but, by themselves, similarities with
arithmetical, iconographic and technological traits in southern Asia
do not amount to a coherent pattern and can easily be explained
away. On the other hand, there is clear evidence for northward
diffusion of agriculture to North America and vague evidence of
ideas from Mexico in the late prehispanic Mississippian culture.
Generally, however, diffusionist interpretations of history have been
out of fashion, partly because they seem to impugn the creativity
of receiving peoples.

More difficult is to sort out political and symbolic factors.
One approach, functionalism, analyses them, alongside sociol-
ogy and economics, as facets of systems which tend to seek
balance. Thus, in *Ancient Mesoamerica*, Blanton and colleagues
argue that the three key factors up to the time of the Spanish
Conquest were scale of society and economy, complexity of
social and political organization, and integration between institutions. In this way, changes in population, for example, can be
understood as effects produced within the system. On the other
hand, the marxist tradition in Mexican social science explains

change as the effect not of general social functions but of struggle between distinct groups of people. Certainly, that is compatible with Mesoamerica's oscillating pattern of unity and fragmentation up to the European period. Another approach explains history as the product of customs and attitudes, arguing, for instance, that decisions such as the timing of Maya battles or the Aztec attitude to the Spaniards were fatalistic. More recently, sceptical about invisible social and cultural forces, there has been a movement to identify the decisions of particular people. It has been encouraged by progress in deciphering Maya royal histories of the mid first millennium AD; but those histories say nothing about most ordinary people. Studies of living communities have had more success in demonstrating the efficacy of people's actions ('agency') in daily life.

Do ordinary people matter in the longer run? There were periods, from about 1000 BC, when 'chiefs' seem to have been the sufficient cause of events; but it looks too as though there were times when the Indians struck them down or simply walked away. For the village was never wholly superseded. This is especially clear from the archaeology of settlement patterns, which provides strong clues about people's access to each other for friendship or labour, their dependence, interdependence, independence or perhaps oppositions (compare *Ancient Mesoamerica*).

If thought and social oganization are related, different kinds of history may be needed for different periods or different communities. Yet this book attempts to make a single story of the whole Mesoamerican experience. What, then, are the sources of evidence? They include living communities, historical archives, archaeology, and art history.

Villages maintaining Native languages today, and, with them, philosophy and many ancient stories, customs and techniques, offer major insights, although it is always difficult for the anthropologists who study them to know how much difference modern history has made. One problem is explained by Rigoberta Menchú: 'We Indians . . . must hide so much in order to preserve our . . . culture.'

For modern history, archives are the main source, of course. The records of the Spanish empire, both in Spain and in Mexico and Central America, are voluminous, much of them yet to be fully investigated. Also remaining to be studied are most of the Indians' own local archives – many hidden for the reason that Miss Menchú explains. Well known, on the other hand, are certain early Colonial 'chronicles', especially the immense output of Friar Bernardino de Sahagún on Aztec life and thought.

Then there are prehispanic records. The earliest evidence for writing may be either a stone found near San Lorenzo Tenochtitlan, possibly dated to the ninth century BC, or the motifs found at Tantoc (Tamtoc), perhaps from about 700 BC, or else the motifs on a cylinder seal found at San Andrés, assigned to the seventh century BC; but the first coherent records known are the Zapotecs', which, carved on stone monuments, seem to describe public affairs from about 500 BC on. There are Mixtec books about history and religion, thought to date from shortly before the Spanish Conquest; and there are books and inscriptions on stone from Central Mexico, including the Aztecs'. The most developed writing system was that of the Maya, best known from inscriptions dating from about AD 300 to 900, describing various aristocratic activities and preoccupations (3). The earliest distinct glyphs date from 400 BC; a short text of the third century BC at San Bartolo remains undeciphered. Other precursors are from west of the Maya region. In a language now identified as early Zoquean but with several glyphs similar to later Maya, a grand stela (stele, decorated or inscribed standing stone) found at La Mojarra (and displayed at the superb Museum of Anthropology in Xalapa) recounts deeds of one, Harvest Mountain Lord, apparently dated, by the Long Count, to AD 143 and 156. Both the account and the accompanying picture of a heavily bedecked grandee prefigure Maya conventions. The other finds appear to date from 36 BC, at Chiapa de Corzo, to AD 162, at Tres Zapotes. Note (again; pp. 15-6) the isthmian distribution of these sites (1). The three or four prehispanic Maya books are devoted to astronomy, astrology and rites. There have been rapid advances in decipherment but big difficulties remain. For example, certain apparently important words seem to remain unchanged for many centuries, and even to today; but, while the form of a phrase remains constant, its meaning and contexts of use may change; and it is often difficult to know from the site of discovery what the original context of a given text was.

Most of the evidence for Mesoamerica's long history is archaeo-logical, materials preserved on or in the ground or in water. New discoveries are being made all the time; but how are they inter-preted? It depends on assumptions about both the samples recov-ered and the original meanings of things. For instance, in order to understand how people lived with each other, it is necessary to know how many they were. To work that out from measurements of areas occupied is difficult; and, even where the remains of houses can be counted, it depends on assumptions about both how many people lived in each and how many of the houses were inhabited at once. As to meaning, art historians are ingenious at interpreting images (iconography) but the strictures about form and context apply just as much as to writing. With the Ball Game, for example, is general knowledge of long repeated and widely distributed built forms and sculptures adequate or is it necessary to know the rules of play and the meanings attributed to them by one people and another in different times?

The difficulties proliferate in defining peoples and traditions. Historians talk of Maya history through two millennia to the Spanish Conquest and continuing to this day; but they define the Toltecs as a tradition of about three centuries and distinguish it from the Aztecs, who were very similar and lasted only two. The Toltecs may have been a distinct and especially energetic nation but the archaeological evidence for them can be seen as just an aristocratic style of art and crafts. Again, the Aztecs called the people beyond Mesoamerica's north frontier Chichimecs – barbarians – but distinguished those who showed signs of 'civilization' from 'real Chichimecs'.

What, then, of the Colonial period and since, when so many Mesoamericans forsook their parents' languages and customs? What of men who liken new jobs in towns to their fathers' traditional toil in the fields? Or what of the new diaspora communities in the USA or people of mixed ancestry in Mexico City, California and Texas, earnestly taking Nahuatl up and trying to revive ancient customs? What is Mesoamerica?

The roots

The first inhabitants were much like the earliest pioneers nearly everywhere else in the Americas. So when did Mesoamerican culture develop, and how (5)? Most scholars consider that it emerged with settled life and farming in about 2000 BC (6). Were the previous 10-20,000 years a gradual prelude, then, or was there a distinct phase of formation?

Both of the best known Native accounts imply that Mesoamerica emerged in a distinct and relatively late phase. The Popol Vuh tells of how the spirits created, first, the animals and then had to try two times over before, at last, they fashioned people. The Aztec Legend of the Suns told of a succession of four races, spanning 2038 years, before the gods brought forth the present world or Sun in AD 1073. Both these stories describe a pattern of progress but they hardly serve as sources for a history that Europeans can understand.

EARLY INHABITANTS

The question of the earliest occupation and the ancestral way of life is part of the wider problem of whence, when and how the Americas as a whole were first colonized. Native Americans are biologically related to the peoples of north-east Asia (7, plates 1,32). Cautious archaeologists long insisted that the earliest sound evidence for people beyond Alaska is a type of hunting equipment first found near Clovis, New Mexico, and in Arizona, and dated to about 13,000 years ago. Now they also accept evidence for occupation at Monte Verde, in Chile, 1000 years earlier; and several other

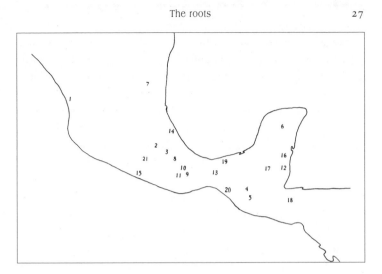

6 Paleoindian and Archaic archaeology: 1 El Calón; 2 Tlapacoya, Zohapilco; 3
Hueyatlaco, Valsequillo; 4 Huehuetenango; 5 Los Tapiales; 6 Loltun; 7 Cañón
Diablo (Tamaulipas); 8 Coxcatlán Cave (Tehuacán Valley); 9 Guilá Naquitz; 10
Yuzanú; 11 Gheo Shih; 12 Belize River; 13 Santa Marta; 14 Santa Luisa; 15
Puerto Marqués; 16 Cobweb Swamp, K'axob; 17 Lake Petenxil; 18 Lake Yojoa;
19 San Andrés; 20 Vuelta Limón; 21 Xihuatoxtla

sites in both South and North America have yielded evidence of
like antiquity. So Mexico and Guatemala must have been occupied by then too; and, indeed, skeletons from near Mexico City
and from underwater caves on Mexico's Caribbean coast have
recently been dated to perhaps 13,000 years ago. Artefacts have
been assigned to as much as 30,000 years ago and more but, for
various technical reasons, these claims are difficult to accept. The
latest candidate for that antiquity is footprints from the Valsequillo
neighbourhood, near Puebla City, where, indeed, 40 years earlier, stone tools unearthed were estimated at 14,000-35,000 years
old. More widely accepted is Tlapacoya, where hearths and stone
implements seem to have dated from some 24,000 years ago.

The most distinctive implement found near Clovis was the
elegant stone point of a spear or dart. Similar ones have been
recovered in Mexico and Central America. In the Valley of Mexico,
they were found among the bones of mammoth which had been

cornered, browsing and drinking at lakesides, or which had been driven there, where they were hampered in bog. The butchered bones of mastodon and horse have been found at a similar site at Huehuetenango and at Hueyatlaco, and those of horse at Loltun. To despatch animals so capable of defending themselves would have entailed co-operation among teams of hunters; and, certainly, the carcasses could have fed many people.

It has been suggested that the rate at which people first spread through the Americas was determined by extermination of their prey. This idea arises partly because the stone points survive better than most of the rest of the early tool kit and are the easiest items for archaeologists to recognize. A more diverse set of implements was found among the remains of a small camp at Los Tapiales, one of more than a hundred discoveries from about 10,000 years ago in and around the K'ich'e basin. The finds included spear or dart points but most of the other equipment was probably for working wood.

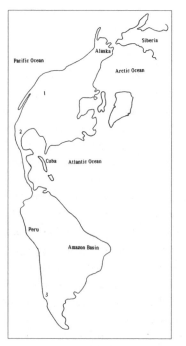

7 Colonization: Native Americans first arrived through Alaska from Siberia. 1 Clovis; 2 Tlapacoya; 3 Monte Verde

The main problem with the remotest period is scarcity of evidence. For, in the Americas, as everywhere else in the world at that time, population was very low. Failing earlier ancestors, is there evidence of Mesoamerican ways in the Archaic period?

Anthropologists' observations of recent 'hunter-gatherer' groups, in the Americas and other continents, led archaeologists to suppose that, during the Archaic, and before, the basic social units, throughout the Americas, were 'bands' of several hundred people. Political leadership among bands is weak; it is not needed for most purposes. Possessions are few but time is abundant. Bushcraft is highly refined. For much of the year, bands disperse, just a few adults together with their dependants, moving from place to place in pursuit of seasonal resources; but larger groups assemble more or less regularly, when and where resources allow or encourage, to exchange news, to meet friends and find spouses, and to perform ceremonies. The distribution of bands is more or less constant but individuals can switch from one to another.

Who would change such a life? By any reckoning, the Archaic lasted 5000 years; and archaeologists sceptical about a distinct 'Hunters' phase before must allow at least 2000 more. Yet changes did take place in Mexico and Upper Central America that were eventually to produce quite a different life. For most prehistorians, that transformation is the emergence of Mesoamerica. The critical factors are settlement (sedentism) and the cultivation of gardens.

SETTLING DOWN

However much they contributed to the larder, hunters adapted to the milder conditions at the end of the Ice Age. As the vegetation changed, big game gave way to migratory herds of antelope and horse and to jack rabbits, succeeded, in turn, by smaller groups of residential whitetail deer and by cottontail rabbits. Food bones from Coxcatlán Cave confirm corresponding changes of diet (plate 2). The size and seasonal mobility of hunting parties must have diminished accordingly – although the amounts of cottontail bones found by archaeologists suggest that many people co-operated to trap rabbits. Smaller stone points were developed, probably for darts cast with a spear thrower.

Yet discoveries in Cañón Diablo (Tamaulipas), and in the Tehuacán Valley, indicate a technology, by 7000 BC, that comprised much more than just hunting – a pattern familiar to archaeologists in western North America, who call it Desert Culture. There were baskets, presumably for collecting plants, and implements for grinding seeds and other tough plant parts. Whether because the preparation was inadequate or on account of chips spalling from the utensils into their pottages and porridges, people's teeth suffered.

One of the strongest responses to warming climate was among colonies of shellfish. As elsewhere in the world, immense coastal mounds of discarded shells show how people latched onto the new resources. The significance for later history is not that so much fish was eaten but that, in a diverse diet, it was reliably and easily collectible through more than half of the year. A great variety of resources was still gathered and hunted from base camps inland such as Santa Luisa and Vuelta Limón, but the seafood was conducive to keeping camps by coasts and estuaries. At El Calón, shells were used to build an immense platform; and the earliest pottery – too brittle for the mobile life – has been recovered from another of these sites, Puerto Marqués (about 2500 BC). Many such sites must have been lost to rising sea levels – a process continuing well beyond the Ice Age – and to silting around river mouths.

In the highlands, Zohapilco, dated to 6000-4500 BC, has yielded the bones both of migratory fowl and of fish, birds and reptiles resident in and around the adjacent lake year round. By implication from these and from the remains of plants, the people may have been permanently settled, which was unusual in the highlands at this time. Tantalising implications arise from the discovery of a well in the Tehuacán Valley dated to the end of the Paleoindian period or the early Archaic: that this feature, 5m deep, was maintained for 4000 years implies organization of labour and perhaps territorial stability.

Some of the social consequences of more sedentary life were recorded by R.S. MacNeish. Along the Belize Valley, his teams collected stone tools apparently dating from all phases of the Archaic. The quantities suggest that, from about 8000 BC, population was rising. At the same time, the distribution of occupation changed. The tools which appear to be earliest were found mostly in small scatters; those dated to the middle of the Archaic were in both small scatters and some larger spreads; and most of those dated to the later part of the period were in larger spreads. Moreover, while, earlier, the bands seem to have moved upriver during the rains and to the coast during the dry season, later, more of the population stayed at or closer to the coast for more of the year. MacNeish detected equivalent trends in Tamaulipas and the Tehuacán Valley. Assuming that he did find a representative sample of the sites, and that the dating is accurate enough, these discoveries not only confirm that people gradually stayed put more but also show that they came to stay together in larger groups. On the other hand, there is evidence for traffic of shells from the Gulf of Mexico in the Tehuacán Valley and of mountain obsidian (stone used for making cutting implements) on coasts, as though long distance exchange compensated for diminished travel – a pattern familiar from the same period elsewhere in the world.

New social opportunities and constraints were developing; and so too must have been norms and customs for guiding people as to who was whose, or what respect and duties were due from who to whom. One means of expressing these ties is formal ritual. Such may have been the purpose of two rows of boulders marking a clearing of 140m² amid an extensive scatter of remains at Gheo Shih – perhaps an early version of a ball court.

One archaeological method for investigating social organization is the analysis of burials. Two graves were found in Coxcatlán Cave. One was of a man, a young woman, and a child, and the other was of a pair of children. The bodies were wrapped in blankets and nets and placed in baskets. The skull of the child with the adults had been smashed, apparently on purpose. Another burial was found in the Santa Marta rockshelter, comprising three bodies, with a fourth stretched out above them, all covered with quern stones. The rites were bold but they did not necessarily involve many people.

GARDEN ATTRACTIONS

Diminishing mobility and rising population were probably directly related. The mobile way of life is hard on expectant mothers and young children. Other things being equal, birth rate and child survival are higher in settlements. Yet, except in rich environments such as the Valley of Mexico, how could people have gathered enough food without moving, in the ancient way, from one seasonal resource to another?

For that question too, MacNeish found an answer. Responding to research in the Middle East – and, through that, to the evolutionary theory of Gordon Childe – he set out to explain the development of complex society in the Americas, 'the rise of civilization' here, by reference to agriculture. He decided to seek the food itself in caves where remains, in storage pits, on floors, or in faeces, were protected from the elements. His strategy succeeded, first in the mountains of Tamaulipas and then, more fully, in the Tehuacán Valley. By investigating various parts of the Valley, MacNeish identified a series of phases through which plants increased as a proportion of the diet while meat diminished. For the Paleoindian period and the earlier part of the Archaic, he claimed also to have shown that, during the dry season, people hunted and gathered in small parties – such as the group buried later in the Coxcatlán cave, perhaps – moving out to the slopes to harvest nuts and seeds as they ripened, and back into the middle of the valley during the rains. Where seeds, acorns, or pods of mesquite were abundant but prone to fall promptly when ripe, several parties would have camped together. Subject, again, to provisos about his sample of sites, this reconstruction makes sense; and it is corroborated, broadly, by evidence from the Valley of Oaxaca, including Gheo Shih.

The finds show that diet gradually diversified and that, while the proportion of cultivated plants increased, that of wild plants diminished. Stone pestles and grinders, and the quern and quernstone – 'mano y metate', standard kitchen equipment until recent generations – were developed for breaking down the plants' protective husks; but, at the same time, with cultivation came domestication and selection, in many plants, for characteristics convenient to farmers and cooks.

Cultivation must have begun on a seasonal basis as gatherers protected natural stands of useful plants from the increasing density and variety of competing vegetation. The longer that people occupied particular sites, the more controlled would these plots have become;

and the more reliable the plot, the more useful among the array of their resources. Not that there was necessarily much planning in this: K.V. Flannery has pointed out that squash, for instance, though later a staple, was probably regarded as merely a harmless weed at first. Other plants, such as a runner bean found at Guilá Naquitz, have since become extinct. Nor was the gardening just for food. Maguey may have been an early cultigen; pits found at Yuzanú could have been used for cooking the edible hearts; and nets, sandals and textiles were woven from the fibre. By the first millenium BC, this sturdy plant may have been vital for amplifying the economy at cooler altitudes in Central Mexico. Gourds were certainly cultivated early: they are not edible but were probably hollowed out to make bottles (of a kind still used today) or fishing floats. Chili was domesticated early too – however tough these folk, that cannot have been a staple!

Just as shells and obsidian were carried between districts, the ecology of one plant and another implies that gardeners exchanged crops and adapted them. Early cotton found in the Tehuacán Valley, for example, is unlikely to have been grown there. Both the repertoire of plants and their yields increased gradually to about 3500 BC, when the process sped up. Eventually, the farmers developed several crops, including maize, tomatoes, avocados and cacao, as well as marigolds and dahlias, enjoyed the world over since spread by the Spanish.

The botanical evidence is corroborated and refined by chemical analysis of bones from burials of successive periods in the Tehuacán Valley. They confirm that there was an accelerating shift to plant foods. The pattern must be due mainly to increasing consumption of grain.

It is generally considered that the shift was thanks to gardening, not collecting from the wild. Although botanists have long pointed to the valleys of southwestern Mexico as the likely origin of maize, it was not until 2008 that soil and stone kitchen tools were found at the Xihuatoxtla rock shelter preserving microscopic traces of maize and squash from the early 6000s BC. From the Gulf coast, pollen from San Andrés may indicate clearing of forest and the introduction of a crop like maize by 5000 BC; and, from about 4600 BC, there was also a trace of manioc (cassava). Maize from Guilá Naquitz has now been dated to 700 years later, apparently some 700 years before its appearance in the Tehuacán Valley (2700 uncalibrated 'radiocarbon years' BC). It sounds like a story of steady diffusion. The crop has been detected in the Amazon basin and Lower Central America with dates back to 5000 BC. It could have been diffused from Mexico; but, by then, manioc may have been grown in the Amazon and Orinoco basins too. There are indications of manioc from Belize and Santa Luisa by 3000 BC and strong evidence that it had reached southern Guatemala by 1750 BC. Did manioc gardens contribute to coastal sedentism?

The issues are made harder by doubts over the genetic prehistory of maize. The general opinion is that it developed from teosinte, which is still found wild in the highlands of Mexico. The evidence is complicated because maize was soon transformed by cultivation; and subsequent crossing with South American varieties has obscured the matter more. No evidence of teosinte was found at Xihuatoxtla, so the story is being pushed well back into the Archaic period.

Whatever the case, maize is an artefact. Whether by chance or by design, management of the plant seems to have selected for several mutations. One of them produced seeds that stuck 'on the cob'. Loss of capacity to disperse them once ripe hampered reproduction in the wild and would have made the plant either prone to collectors and, or, attractive to cultivators. Pollen preserved in sediments beneath Cobweb Swamp, Lake Yojoa and Lake Petenxil records increasing use of maize during the third millennium BC. Yet the first ears were hardly an inch long and the seeds not only tiny but also covered with hard skins. Again, horticultural selection may have been at work, but not until after 2000 BC were the seed cases soft enough and the seeds themselves big enough and numerous enough to become Mesoamerica's mainstay. Thenceforth, though, maize and men came to depend on each other and development of the crop has continued to this day. Other crops underwent equivalent changes. In the Middle East, the shift to grains was quicker partly because the botanical transformations were simpler.

From 2000 BC on, increasing proportions of the acreage once used for gathering and hunting diverse resources from the wild were turned into concentrated patches of maize, beans and squash under close control. These favourites may, indeed, have been selected from the wild as 'companion plants' (*8*): maize is chemically protected from weeds and insects by squash and beans; its demand on soil nitrogen is offset by beans; and squash leaves protect the soil from evaporation and erosion. Moreover, by planting the 'triumvirate' together, farmers raise yield and spread the risk of particular crops failing. The routines of growing them in plots that are shifted between fallows ('slash & burn' or swidden cultivation, commonly called 'milpa' in Mesoamerica) became images for thinking, to this day, about all life (*9, plates 3, 4*).

Maize is rich in starch, carbohydrates and oil, and also in thiamine and vitamin A; but its dietary success depended too on a mineral and the two companion plants. Soaking the seeds with lime or wood ash – a mixture called nixtamal in Central Mexico – makes it yet easier to remove their outer skin and it also stimulates release of more protein, while the lime contributes calcium. Finds in southern Guatemala show that the preparation was used by 1200 BC. Then, when maize is digested with beans, rich in protein and lysine, and with squash, the nutritional value of each is enhanced, and they comprise a viable diet by

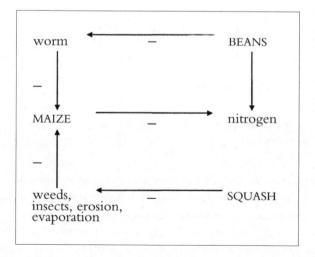

8 A 'triumvirate' of 'companion plants'

month	task	rite etc.	remark
February March		offer to Seed and Rain; Carnival	
April		fertility	
May	clear milpa plot; burn; sow	best Monday, Wednesday or Saturday	machete
June July	scare birds; weed; tend soil		
August	weed; tend soil		
September October	scare birds; weed; pick young ears		
November December	harvest; double; carry; pile corn	All Souls solstice, Earth fertility spirit	appease 'winds' birth

month	task	rite etc.	remark
October	measure and cut plot		new plot: orient with Sun
April	burn and remeasure	offer to Wind Lords	measure 13x2 paces in order
May		Call Rain	rains later now
June	sow		
July	weed		
October	pick young ears; double	offer to Wind Lords	
November December	harvest	All Souls	

9 The cycle of maize: comparing the upper chart, of Nahuas in Central Mexico, with the lower, Maya in the Yucatan peninsula, shows environmental variation ('doubling' bends the ears to dry, discourages weevils and encourages growing beans)

themselves (*10*; though chili enhances the taste no end!). Squashes were among the first crops, while common beans and tepary beans were eaten as early as maize. The chemistry of bones from burials at K'axob dating between the ninth century BC and the ninth AD indicates that maize made up 30 per cent of the diet and meat or fish 10 per cent.

diet	weight	note
maize	500 g	nixtamal
beans	100 g	protein, lysine
squash	50 g	
tomato	50 g	
chili	20 g	Vitamins A & C
nutrition	**value**	**comparison**
energy	2177 kcal	2200 kcal
protein	6700 mg	DRI 4100 mg
calcium	217 mg	DRI 900 mg
phosphorus	1069 mg	DRI 700 mg
Vitamin A	1.6 mg	DRI 0.8 mg
thiamine	3.2 mg	DRI 1.1 mg
riboflavin	0.8 mg	DRI 1.2 mg
niacin	13.6 mg	DRI 15 mg
Vitamin C	117 mg	DRI 87 mg

10 Value of a hypothetical Aztec adult daily diet compared to average energy consumed in Guatemala today and Dietary Reference Intakes (DRI, equivalent to RDA)

However, present archaeological evidence suggests that beans remained a minor food well into the Formative period and that protein came from small amounts of game, duck and other wild animals, and from the two domesticates, turkey and, more importantly, dog. Nor, today, can rural families always count on harvesting enough to keep them in beans through the whole year.

Another reason for the success of grain and beans was that, once harvested and dried, both are stored easily. In the highlands, caves and pits had long been used to bank surpluses gathered in case of fluctuations in supply, which are more marked than at lower altitudes. Not only did storage enable people to stay longer in particular places but also, like growing crops, it must have encouraged settlement, for stores had to be guarded. Larger stores and bigger fields could support more people; so then yet bigger fields would have been needed ... At the same time, the pattern of crops diffused to the North American Southwest and South, with comparable effects there later.

ARCHAIC HERITAGE

Language too provides clues about Archaic history. Distinctions
tend to arise as communication between groups declines. As an
effect of diminishing mobility and, or, the development of speech
communities of a critical size, Zapotec and Chatino, for example,
are thought to have diverged from Mixtec and Cuicatec during the
third and fourth millennia BC. The Popol Vuh explains that, once,
everyone spoke the same tongue. Affinities among their languages
today imply that all Maya did, indeed, speak alike until the later
third millennium BC.

Whoever first developed agriculture, the basic issue is as to
why gardening and farming were taken up or how the technology
fitted the social requirements of the time. For, while production of
food and rising population reinforced each other, it was customs
and institutions that determined what was feasible or acceptable.
Noting finds, in the Tehuacán Valley, of quids of its stalks and other
sugary parts, as well as later evidence of beer and wine, an argument
for 'Sweet beginnings' in domestication suggests that maize became
a sociable medium for consensus. Did Mesoamericans sozzle themselves into the hierarchies of the Formative period?

Basic techniques of farming changed little after the Archaic.
Perhaps general features of Mesoamerican philosophy and religion
too were formed in that era. So much of the sensitivity of later farmers to the seasons, the lie of the land, and the soil would have been
at least as critical for hunter-gatherers. The intense value placed on
maize during the past 2000 years would have been appropriate during
the late Archaic too; and gathering of wild resources continued well
into the Formative. Indeed, the image of the Archaic fascinated the
Aztecs. According to one of their myths of origin, people living under
previous Suns ate primitive varieties of corn. Clearly, more research
is needed on the later part of the Archaic period; but most scholars
consider that Mesoamerican culture crystallized around institutions
that developed only at the close of the Archaic. Certainly, the pace
of history quickened during the second millennium BC. The old life
was left around the Chichimec fringe, to the north.

3

The Olmec phase

The two millennia from about 1800 BC witnessed rising population and development of new forms of social organization (5).
By the later part of this period, the Formative, Mesoamerica was a
world of pyramids and all that they suggest of both society and worship.

No one factor – population, physical environment, technology,
political organization, or religion and 'world view' – can be distinguished as most basic for the 'rise of civilization'. They fed into each
other, one stimulating development, another dampening or diverting
it. In places, no doubt, particular factors were critical; but one telling
feature of the process in Mesoamerica was exchange between regions.
Telling too, though, is the evidence of rapid social changes and reversals; Formative chieftains were not always assured of their power.

The present chapter takes the story up to about 500 BC. By then,
distinct peoples had their own languages, customs and histories. The
most famous 'civilization' is 'the Olmecs' but, although they are often
dubbed Mesoamerica's 'mother culture', they were probably not a
single people.

VILLAGES RANKED

In one region and another, the number and the size of settlements
increased during the Formative period (11). The trend had probably
started in the Archaic but it could not have continued without
reorganizing the 'face to face' social relations of the time. In places,
that was achieved by allowing distinct ranks to emerge among villagers. Much the same took place in many other parts of the world.

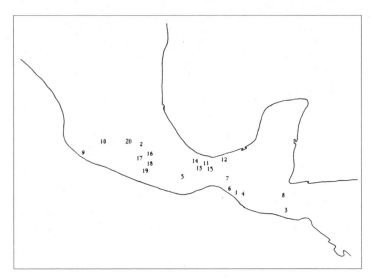

11 The Early and Middle Formative periods: 1 Paso de la Amada, Cantón
Corralito, Izapa, La Blanca; 2 Coapexco, Loma Torremote, Tlapacoya, Tlatilco,
Zacatenco; 3 Chalchuapa; 4 Abaj Tak'alik'; 5 Huitzo, Mazaltepec, San José
Mogote, Santo Domingo Tomaltepec, Tierras Largas; 6 Laguna Zope; 7 Chiapa
de Corzo; 8 Copan; 9 Capacha; 10 El Opeño; 11 San Lorenzo Tenochtitlan; 12
La Venta, San Andrés; 13 Laguna de los Cerros; 14 Tres Zapotes; 15 El Manatí; 16
Chalcatzingo; 17 Teopantecuanitlan; 18 Oxtotitlan; 19 Juxtlahuaca; 20 Chupícuaro

Survey in the Valley of Oaxaca has shown that the earliest permanent settlements comprised about ten loosely scattered little
homesteads. No doubt they were connected to each other and to
other such groups as kin, but each presumably had its own garden.
Produce was stored in pits around the dwellings and, although plant
remains and bones recovered here, from contemporary sites in the
Tehuacán Valley, and elsewhere, show that the ancient techniques of
gathering and hunting still provided half of the food, the volume
of storage was higher than in the Archaic period. In the Valley of
Mexico too, hunting, fowling and fishing long remained important. However, in less abundant environments, the fields accounted
sooner for more of the larder. Prof. Flannery and colleagues have
argued that the yield of maize had reached a threshold at which it
rewarded more exclusive husbandry.

Along the southern Pacific coast, in Soconusco, substantial communities had settled together for much of the year since the later Archaic. Permanent villages of up to 200 people were established by 1800 BC. Scatters of the distinctive pottery of the following centuries show that a few of them grew yet larger and, by 1400 BC, one, Paso de la Amada, had gathered at least a quarter of the whole district's population, some 2000 people. It appears to have been planned out with a large plaza and a ball court, the earliest yet discovered in Mesoamerica. Workshops seem to have been located near the better appointed houses. In the middle of the village, overlooking the plaza, stood a hall. Rebuilt several times, it gradually rose on its platform. Inside were several fireplaces. They are the subject of speculation. For council fires would be compatible with decisions reached collectively; but if they were domestic hearths, then the hall may have been the seat of a dynasty of chieftains who indebted the villagers by sponsoring feasts – a common custom in recent centuries. Among the finds in the district are figurines of fat men with distinctive headgear and ornaments, intended, perhaps, to remind people of their chiefs.

For farming may have demanded co-operation. By the mid first millennium BC, most villages in the Valley of Oaxaca lay within a short walk of irrigable land; and traces of irrigation have been found in Mexico City and near Puebla City. Local irrigation does not necessarily demand large-scale organization but the pattern may indicate collective management. There were also problems to cope with.

Even as they gained control over selected plants, by eliminating other species as weeds and pests, farmers risked famine should the favourites perish in field or store. Another danger is illustrated by the Valley of Mexico. Population here was growing very quickly. Coapexco probably had more than 500 people, and Tlapacoya and Tlatilco may have been even bigger. Whether or not on account of boom or bust in their homeland, many of the villagers were probably immigrants from Morelos, to the south: most settlement was in the southern part of the Valley, and the earliest pottery was akin to wares from Morelos. Although early harvests may have been copious, the method was unsustainable: fierce soil erosion was taking place. Growth did continue but most hillside settlements shifted to the shores of the lake; and erosion declined. Zacatenco is typical of the new regime: hunting and fowling remained important here well beyond 1000 BC.

The Valley of Oaxaca illustrates other economic and political patterns. In the single-roomed houses of the early Formative, distinct activities seem to have taken place, kitchen tasks on one side, craft work on another. Techniques for knapping flint tended to vary between groups of houses, and while some households evidently specialized in working iron ore, others preferred stone or shell. Specialization has been recorded among the remains of houses at Chalchuapa and in Honduras too.

Now, some of these materials had to be imported. The villages of Soconusco brought minerals from as far as 500km. Shells were carried to Oaxaca from the Gulf of Mexico. Pottery came in from there too and from Soconusco and Morelos; and, equally, pottery from Oaxaca or in Oaxaca style has been found in other parts of Mexico (see below). The distribution of obsidian is telling too. Collective supply began in the larger village of San José Mogote, from about 1000 BC, and then, by 800 BC, in surrounding settlements. Where, earlier, various sources were used, households now shared single sources. A couple of centuries later, collective supply began in the Valley of Mexico too: at Loma Torremote, one bigger house seems to have served as both the workshop for stone implements and the distributory.

Thus, whether or not with popular consent, coalescence of villages could have been prompted by demands of chiefs, development of crafts, need for co-operation in the fields, and, or, variations in farmers' prosperity. By the early first millennium BC, houses showed disparities in the work invested on the buildings themselves, in the deer bones left, presumably, from eating venison, and in the amounts of materials or more elaborately wrought goods brought, presumably at greater cost, from other districts. By the middle of the millennium, a minority boasted finer crockery than their neighbours'. The big house at Loma Torremote had the largest stores of grain; and the main shrine in the vicinity lay near by. Other clusters of households may have had their own shrines; but it looks as though there was collective worship. Leading households may have sponsored public rites and fed dependants or visitors from their stores on festive occasions. No doubt clientage and patronage were negotiated, and perhaps the Ball Game was played on such occasions at Paso de la Amada.

Defence too may have encouraged people to settle together. It was in about 600 BC, according to the excavators, that a slab was laid on San José Mogote's central platform, carved with the figure of a mutilated corpse – perhaps a victim of battle. A pair of accompanying signs has been read as a date or the victim's name (see p.13). At about the same time, the adjacent temple burned down. By analogy from Aztec warfare, it could have been targeted by an enemy as Mogote's heart (28). One site, Mazaltepec, may have been defended as early as 600 BC, overlooking a route into the Valley from the west. On the other hand, at that time, the Valley was divided into three zones: Mogote's was the most populous but it may have faced rivalry from the others. Whatever the case, its temple seems to have been replaced, by 500 BC, not with another shrine but by a mansion. Does political power spring from leadership in war?

The villages in Soconusco were surrounded by enough land for their respective fields and for supplying water, wood and supplementary wild foods; but disparities of size and distinct features of layout suggest different and complementary local roles. Likewise, in the Valley of Oaxaca, San José Mogote had grown much bigger than other settlements by 1300 BC and, three centuries later, there were other larger villages but Mogote had grown yet more. The bigger places had central plazas (squares) and larger buildings, including temples. The pattern looks like a 'settlement hierarchy' in which people in the larger places provide satellites with services such as council facilities, rites or markets. Inhabitants of the smaller villages must have contributed both to local public works and the programme of building in Mogote. There were three tiers of places, Mogote at the top – ten times bigger than any other by 600 BC – and hamlets at the bottom.

By then, population growth and political development was accelerating in many districts. Among San José Mogote's possible enemies in the west, and in the Puebla basin, villages were arranging themselves in tiers. Paso de la Amada had been superseded by Cantón Corralito, and a similar pattern has been discovered along the coastal plains to east, centred on La Blanca, and west, centred on Laguna Zope, as well as inland, centred on Chiapa de Corzo. At many of these places has been found the distinctive art of the Olmecs (see below). By now too, the first of the great Maya pyramids had already been built (chapter 5).

CEMETERIES

Burials too can yield evidence of political organization. Untold numbers have been disturbed by treasure hunters; but some cemeteries or groups of burials have escaped vandalism and been recorded by archaeologists. It is difficult to understand the symbolism of ancient rites, but treatment of the dead and selection of goods to accompany them were, of course, discretionary so they may express ideas and intentions more explicitly than do subsistence and settlement.

That the commonest burial place was beneath the floors of dwellings or in the surrounding yards implies that the household maintained its own sense of identity and, hence, that to gather people into villages could have been felt as a threat to families. For lack of evidence for temples, some archaeologists consider that the many little pottery figurines accompanying burials in the earlier part of the Formative period confirm that the household was the centre of worship. Perhaps the figurines represented ancestors; and perhaps Soconusco chieftains sought to impose themselves on local genealogies with their chubby figurines.

Various rites of burial have been recorded in the Valley of Oaxaca. Most bodies were stretched out but some skeletons are flexed, as though the corpse had been swathed. The former were provided with just a few goods but the latter had more and, or, goods of better quality. Many of the 'richer' burials were covered with stone slabs, moreover, and more of these than the 'poorer' ones were accompanied by other inhumations (compare Santa Marta, chapter 2).

A most interesting discovery in Oaxaca is the decoration on pottery found with burials of men. Where, in some villages – or, at San José Mogote, in parts of the village – motifs interpreted as attributes of a fiery (or perhaps feathered) snake prevail, in others there prevails a 'St Andrew's Cross' form. Like similar motifs on household pottery, these are thought to be Olmec symbols. It remains to be confirmed that the two patterns in the cemeteries are consistently contemporary but it has been suggested, by analogy with later customs in North and South America, that they are emblems for half societies (moieties) with complementary rights and duties. Alternatively, they may represent rival factions.

Two or three larger cemeteries have been investigated elsewhere. The best known was at Tlatilco. The graves seem to have been laid amidst a village (a sample of them is reconstructed in the National Museum of Anthropology, Mexico City). As in Oaxaca, rites and 'wealth' varied. Among those interred with the most goods were children and youths, as though they had inherited social status. Paul Tolstoy has pointed out that, where most of the burials were laid out east-west, a minority lay north-south. Since most of the latter were of teenage or adult men, he argues that they were husbands who married in, that 'home' or family identity tended to be worked out in reference to women, but that husbands retained the distinct rite of their parents. It is interesting, then, that the contemporary village of Coapexco may have been laid out in two rows, like villages with dual organization in North and South America (and see chapter 1).

It is the quality and quantity of the pottery vessels and figurines that has drawn so much attention to Tlatilco. The figurines, in particular, while highly stylized, seem to illustrate everyday life – clothing and coiffure, courtship, mothering, dancing. They also show contortionism, analogous, perhaps, to yoga – or perhaps just a joke; and another theme shows aspects of the Ball Game. Others are equally striking but more difficult to understand: a preoccupation with bodily deformity; and a series of masks displaying features of both life and death – a conceit well rehearsed among later peoples.

Distinct from the rest of the pottery here, at Tlapacoya and Coapexco, and at other cemeteries in the region are forms and motifs in 'Olmec' style. For Tlatilco, Dr Tolstoy has shown that they tend to be associated with women. Similar evidence has been unearthed at Copan, where complementary aspects of the fiery snake motif occur in distinct groups of burials – though, again, it is not known whether they are strictly contemporary. One burial here was accompanied by more than 300 little items of jade – and the skulls of two children.

Another apparently exotic aspect of the pottery repertoire from Tlatilco and several other cemeteries is a range of surface treatments and forms, especially bottles with long necks or bifurcated 'stirrup' spouts and jars and bowls on three or four feet. Slightly earlier wares from Capacha, in western Mexico, had many of the same features, and crypts at El Opeño have yielded similar pottery. Most archaeologists ascribe these resonances to Central Mexico and the Gulf Coast; but a wider view reveals various iconographic similarities between the 'Olmecs' and contemporary art in north-western South America, with a scatter of finds from cemeteries and ceremonial centres in Honduras and the Pacific districts of Central America in between. The jars and bowls are reminiscent of 'Chorreroid' wares in Ecuador. The matter is full of doubt because so many of the finds in western Mexico and to the south were robbed from tombs without archaeological record, and because research on long distance or 'secondary' diffusion has been out of archaeological fashion (chapter 1). Yet there is other evidence for links along the Pacific seaway (chapter 6).

The boldly painted pottery from around Chupícuaro catches the eye in several museums and, presumably, a lot of private collections. Frustratingly little is known about the cemeteries that produced it, let alone the makers' lives, but they have now been assigned to the middle and later part of the first millennium BC.

THE OLMEC MONUMENTS

The southern coast of the Gulf of Mexico is often called the 'Olmec heartland'. Here were the four biggest known places in Mesoamerica between 1450 and 500 BC, along with most of the sculptures which are the Olmecs' most famous hallmark.

'Olmec' is a name assigned by archaeologists. Nobody knows what the inhabitants of those places were called. As to their language, there are two guesses: some form of Maya perhaps once spoken everywhere from Huastec country to Yucatan; or a Mixean language, like Popoloca, which is spoken today in the western part of the 'heartland' – and which may have been spoken in Soconusco too.

The first great Olmec centre was San Lorenzo Tenochtitlan. After a couple of centuries of occupation, San Lorenzo was enlarged, in about 1450 BC, by turning the low hill that it occupied into a vast platform and by building earthen mounds on top of that to form a series of courts. More than 5000 people occupied terraces on the surrounding slopes and more lived in smaller settlements around. The ceremonial zone was dignified with sculptures, including ten of the type known (appropriately enough) as Colossal Heads (plate 5). They may be portraits of chiefs; but many of the statues were either unfinished or defaced and then toppled in about 1200 BC and the ceremonial zone was abandoned. San Lorenzo was reoccupied but then deserted again in about 750 BC. The hinterland declined too. Similar changes took place around Laguna de los Cerros. Archaeological surveys suggest that many people dispersed to the hills.

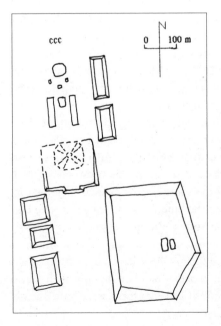

12 La Venta, the central earthworks, the platform in the middle occupied by an eroded pyramid (c marks Colossal Head)

By 750, La Venta had become the principal place in the region. La Venta too comprised courts bounded by earthen platforms; and it has a pyramid. There was also a lot of stone artwork, including Colossal Heads and buried pavements of serpentine. The most elaborate tomb known in all of Formative Mesoamerica was found here. Set at the north end of the main line of earthworks (*12*), it comprised a room built of basalt columns covered by an earthen mound. Accompanied by a set of finely worked jade ornaments, there were two bodies. They were youngsters, accorded such honours through inheritance, presumably, as at Tlatilco (or perhaps not – read on …). At La Venta too, the statues were attacked, in about 350 BC. Much of the sculpture, including the basalt tomb, was rescued from an oil field and installed at the Archaeological Park in Villahermosa.

Two other large sites are known but less investigated. At Laguna de los Cerros, the earthworks have the same orientation as La Venta's. Those of the mainly later site at Tres Zapotes spread almost 3km along a river.

Because much of the coastal plain is forested and marshy (or was until recent development), the settlement pattern remains obscure. Tracks led out from San Lorenzo, and smaller sites have been found near by. They were probably ordinary villages surrounded by fields, but sculptures at some of them, like Potrero Nuevo or Cruz del Milagro, indicate that they may have been the seats of minor chiefs. There were also rural shrines like El Manatí: preserved by gushing springs here were rubber balls – for the Ball Game, perhaps – and other items including ten wooden figurines with the weird 'baby-face' features well known from Olmec pottery; and, in the last phase of deposits, the skeletons, both complete and fragmentary, of infants.

No doubt, festivals were held at the regional centres, with rites among the earthworks and sculptures, at key times of year. Inhabitants and visiting villagers must have watched or joined in. Indeed, they must have been the builders; and, hauled or rafted up to 70 and 120km from their source, the immense blocks of basalt of which most of the sculptures are made may have counted as contributions to the rites. Pilgrims may have come from much further: among imported materials at San Lorenzo has been found pottery in Oaxaca style, while at La Venta there were little mirrors possibly from the Valley of Oaxaca.

Why did the Gulf Coast produce these prodigious places? One suggestion is that burgeoning population in the highlands prompted colonization at the end of the Archaic period. Set out on soils recharged every rainy season by the great rivers, the new farms may have allowed – or encouraged – population to rise. M.D. Coe & R.A. Diehl have suggested that disparities developed between farms on different qualities of soil, giving rise to dependence and patronage. On the other hand, alluviation may have buried the traces of an earlier population that was always denser than the highlanders, perhaps Olmec roots stretched as far back as the gardens at San Andrés. Meanwhile, among the mountains near Tres Zapotes, villagers still gathered food from the wild throughout the Formative period. Nor did they enjoy such wealth as the lowlanders.

There are 'Olmec' settlements elsewhere, although neither as early as San Lorenzo nor as big as the 'heartland' sites. Chalcatzingo lies at the foot of a striking pair of hills. There were a couple of big buildings by 1100 BC but, drawing people in from surrounding hamlets, the village was gradually enlarged and, from 700 to 500 BC, it was provided with monumental architectural features including Olmec decoration, while many of the great boulders that litter the site were carved with Olmec motifs too. One stone bench or 'altar', Monument 22, carved with a monster's face, entombed two burials; and five other bodies were interred in front of it. The most impressive of the rock carvings overlooks the village with long views beyond: a figure is shown seated on a bench in a 'cave', surrounded by rain storms and flourishing maize (plate 6). Here too, sculptures were deliberately broken up. Teopantecuanitlan was a ceremonial centre with a resident population supported by a scheme for damming water and irrigating. In about 900 BC, a court was laid out evidently to mark the passage of the Sun at the March equinox. It was decorated with Olmec images of a jaguar. There was at least one ball court. Several other such places are suspected in the same district. Some details of the layout and ornamentation of buildings in Chalcatzingo and Teopantecuanitlan were shared, and it would be interesting to know if they occur elsewhere too. From the same region came disconcerting 'baby' figurines in Olmec style.

To the south, there are Olmec figures painted in rock shelters and caves. At Oxtotitlan is a brightly coloured figure wearing the beak and feathers of a great bird. He is seated on a bench like Chalcatzingo's Monument 22. More than 1000m under ground at Juxtlahuaca, amongst other images, an imposing man whose costume includes jaguar pelt fittings decorates the wall of a cavern full of human skeletons. Pottery from the Gulf Coast has been found in Oaxaca, and buildings at San José Mogote, Santo Domingo Tomaltepec and Huitzo were oriented on the same axis as the earthworks of La Venta (but a small clearing at Tierras Largas is a local precedent; and Huitzo is earlier than La Venta). In Soconusco, there have been finds of both pottery and sculpture in Olmec style. Some of the pottery came from the Gulf Coast. Survey to the east revealed rapid concentration of population around La Blanca, in about 900 BC. Perhaps prompted by chieftains' demands or by threats from Izapa or Abaj Taka'lik', the development was like Chalcatzingo's and the result a 'settlement hierarchy' like San José Mogote's. La Blanca itself was dominated by a pyramid and at least four secondary mounds. These earthworks are now badly damaged but remains of houses seem to be well preserved, and in two of them were found personal adornments of greenstone. Carvings and sculptures with Olmec motifs have been found at La Blanca, Abaj Tak'alik' and far off at Chalchuapa where there was a pyramid like those at La Blanca and La Venta.

How did places further afield relate to the 'heartland'? Were they the seats of provincial governors, or the headquarters of traders or missionaries? Or was the 'heartland', to the contrary, not the sole source of Olmec ideas? Some archaeologists suspect that the sculptural style originated on the Pacific slopes of the south-east; and some consider that early pottery at San Lorenzo Tenochtitlan is derived from the wares in Soconusco.

PEOPLE OR SYMBOLS?

The usual interpretation of the Olmecs has been that they were a nation who spread their beliefs from the 'heartland' to the rest of

Mesoamerica. This theory is sometimes used to explain the crystallization of Mesoamerica as a culture area. Considering particularly the number of jade carvings in Olmec style from the highlands, some have reasoned that the Olmecs were originally highlanders; but this is the same kind of argument.

On the other hand, the most parsimonious interpretation of the evidence is that 'the Olmecs' was a cult, not a culture. This view allows that the 'heartland Olmecs' were the most populous society or societies of the time, and that they may have been a nation. It allows too that features of the cult probably originated in the Gulf region; but it also allows that other peoples shared, took part in, borrowed from, adapted or contributed to the cult. With this view, of course, it would remain to explain the cult's apparent appeal at that time; and that is the remaining task of the present chapter, to try to explain, first, what the cult was and, then, why it appealed so widely.

What were the monuments for? By comparing them and by selective reference to later historical evidence, provisional readings can be made. Two or three examples can suffice to elucidate the main themes.

Chalcatzingo's carving of the figure in a 'cave' seems to express general Mesoamerican principles of the integration of the cosmos and the claims of chiefs and kings to be pivots of the system (plate 6; the National Anthropology Museum, Mexico City, shows a replica of the composition's central part). From the cave usher volutes like the scrolls in Aztec manuscripts that indicate speech or flowing water (*30* and *38*). By implication, the cave is on the side of a mountain, like the carving itself. The volutes represent water springing directly from the mountain; or the source of the clouds, shown above with heavy drops of rain falling from them; or perhaps thunder rolling from the cave – and, or, the voice of the central figure. Although it is not shown here, the fiery snake shown on pottery in Oaxaca and elsewhere probably belongs to the same set of ideas – it is lightning. Both the figure within and a schematic eye above the upper lip of the cave emphasise that, whether directly or indirectly, it is the mountain personified that provides water for the maize plants shown beneath the clouds and springing directly from the cave's corners. The lashes or brows around the eye look like flames, and the pupil is marked with a St Andrew's cross – again, perhaps, the same motif that is found on pottery in Oaxaca and elsewhere, and in sculpture. As for the central figure, suffice it to point out that a couple of little maize plants spring from the headdress and that an object is held in the arms in the same kind of way as for 'heartland' chieftains also depicted in caves (see below). Thus, 'the king' (as archaeologists call it – some see it as a woman) is engaged with Earth in providing rain, perhaps all across the broad landscape viewed from his shelter there on the hill. The seat that he occupies may be the kind of bench depicted on Monument 22. Was he a figure like Harvest Mountain Lord from La Mojarra (chapter 1)?

Altar 4 from La Venta may be a bench of the same kind again (plate 7). Where 'the king' can only be admired by scrambling up a steep hillside, Altar 4 was probably more accessible. As at Chalcatzingo, the central figure, with headdress, sits in a mouth of the Earth – as witness eyes, lips and teeth above, a St Andrew's cross between the fangs, and maize plants springing from the corners. The bench is shown draped with a jaguar pelt. There is a political statement here as well: cords run from the central figure to smaller figures at the sides. The latter are sometimes interpreted as captives, with the implication that the central figure owed his power to force, but neither does he grasp the cords nor do they bind the lateral figures. Rather, the message is probably about the central figure's ancestry. The 'altar' may represent a tomb sited in order to establish a lineage's dynastic claims to certain lands. At least some Colossal Heads were carved from 'altars', perhaps as memorials.

La Venta's stelae appear to show chiefs' military and perhaps diplomatic roles. They prefigure the La Mojarra stela. Another of the altars seems to show one of the ceremonies that the chieftain or his aides carried out: officiants carry squirming children toward the central figure crouched in a cave/mouth; the child in the central figure's hands is limp. The children feature domed heads, cleft skulls and down-turned lips, characteristics repeated in many other Olmec images. They have been interpreted as the signs of offspring from a woman and a jaguar; but one of the Aztecs' most important rites was the sacrifice of thoroughbred human children to their rain god, and the Olmecs may have done the same (El Manatí). Some consider that the groove in the skull was a symbol for the hole from which sprang the farmer's maize plant. Was that the idea about the children buried at Santa Marta (chapter 2)?

Reviewing the range of Olmec iconography, several scholars have agreed that it is pervaded by themes of transgression or transformation between people and jaguars and eagles. This idea was to haunt Mesoamerica for the rest of the prehispanic period. Indeed, exchange between different forms of life is a shamanic theme that recurs throughout Native American thought. No doubt the theme of fertility and productivity was already widely familiar in Mesomerica; but perhaps the general appeal of Olmec symbolism was that it formulated principles hitherto inchoate. Assessing all the evidence, from the figurines to the cave paintings, art historians have distinguished about half a dozen 'gods'. What was the value of making them explicit?

ETHICAL CRISIS

In contrast to the prevalent view, some scholars have been urging that the Gulf coast was not the sole hearth of Mesoamerican civilization but, rather, that it pioneered a widespread development. The following suggestion uses this idea to argue that the Olmecs solved a common problem (13).

As communities grew larger, people's relationships with each other and the spirits that governed their world was seen as more mediated than before, so that the connection had to be more carefully managed. For, with more selective agriculture and specialization in crafts, co-ordinated labour became critical. Pierre Clastres has described vividly the dilemma in American Indian societies unaccustomed to royalty: the chief can only persuade with goodly words; he cannot order his people. Whether as a functional consequence of economic differentiation and centralization or through calculated manipulation, Olmec doctrine – and perhaps ideology in Soconusco before – vested leaders with sacred roles or attributed sanctity to their words. Children may have been sacrificed as an

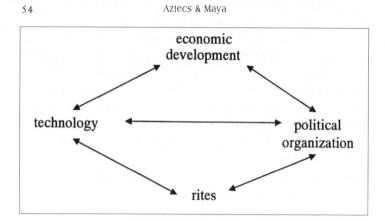

13 The role of ritual among the Olmecs

especially vivid statement of dependence on – or reciprocation with – the spirits. The symbolism and art style was a religious idiom for claims about social standing and political authority.

The distribution of obsidian in Oaxaca could have been achieved by co-operative institutions. Perhaps they were organized in moieties. The ceremonial buildings could have been built with voluntary consensus too – although the gory sculpture at San José Mogote suggests chiefly or priestly command. Yet, taken together, the Olmec evidence, if not the discoveries in Soconusco too, suggests social ranking. As the top echelon acquired distinct powers and privileges, chiefs became kings. Among other contrivances, the Colossal Heads were commissioned to record their virtues and insignia.

Taking part at the great centres, helping to build them, helped to generate and sustain new myths of authority; but were the people 'duped', then? Considering later Mesoamerican ideas about cyclic fortune, destruction of the sculptures could have been ceremonial; or it may have been inflicted by outsiders; or it could be proof of popular rejection, in favour of parochial 'village' affiliations. It would be interesting to know whether the cults were oriented more to domestic affairs or to mobilization against threats perceived from further afield – a question to reappear in the following chapters.

Although uniformity of many Olmec motifs does imply a distinct 'heartland', various forms, techniques and iconographic emphases in the pottery of one region and another suggest that the cult was adapted to local circumstances. However, it is telling that where, at Zacatenco and its neighbours, the economy was less agricultural, there is no evidence for chieftains and little or none for public ritual, nor for that former Olmec interest at Tlatilco.

The Olmecs have commonly been regarded as a catalyst for Mesoamerican history. The view recommended here accords less creativity to any one people. Arguing for responsiveness to Olmec ideas rather than mere acquiescence – that they made sense in one region and another, in various ways – it suggests that a common culture did already exist by the Formative period. One challenge, then, is to find out about late Archaic beliefs. From any point of view, however, the Olmec era was a transition; and the later Formative brought a further transformation.

4

Enigmatic kingdoms

The last five centuries BC witnessed the creation of the state. Following the story up to about AD 700 in western Mesoamerica, this chapter covers the later part of the Formative period and most of the Classic (5).

Archaeological methods for recognizing early states are much as for the chiefdoms considered in the previous chapter. Where, in general, a chiefdom's settlement pattern has two or three tiers, states tend to have at least four. Partly 'disembedded' from traditional rights and duties, the capital was a town where many inhabitants were supported by produce from its hinterland. States' capitals were like the ceremonial centres of chiefdoms, but most were bigger. States had more power to produce and allocate material or symbolic resources and to deploy force at home or abroad. Like chieftains, the governors tended to glorify themselves in rites or myth, and their tombs can often be recognized in the same ways too; but the early rulers of western Mesoamerica are elusive.

The first state was formed in the Valley of Oaxaca. Archaeology and the preliminary decipherment of inscriptions are providing an increasingly rounded and detailed account of the process and of the state's fortunes thereafter. By the third century AD, however, Oaxaca was eclipsed by Teotihuacan which, in due course, affected nearly all Mesoamerica (14). Teotihuacan is the grandest monument of them all – and the most enigmatic.

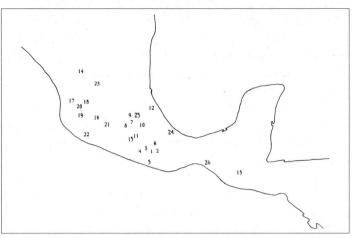

14 The later Formative and earlier Classic periods: 1 Monte Albán, Cuilapan, Hierve el Agua, San José Mogote, Santo Domingo Tomaltepec; 2 Lambityeco, Yegüih, San Martín Tilcajete, Jalieza, El Palmillo; 3 Huachino, Etlatongo; 4 Monte Negro; 5 Cerro de la Cruz, Río Viejo; 6 Quiotepec; 7 Teotihuacan; 8 Cuicuilco; 9 Chingú; 10 Cholula, Tetimpa; 11 San Ignacio; 12 El Tajín; 13 Kaminaljuyu; 14 Alta Vista; 15 Xochicalco; 16 El Opeño; 17 El Arenal; 18 Huitzilapa; 19 Cerro del Agua Escondida; 20 Guachimontón; 21 Tingambato; 22 La Campana; 23 La Quemada; 24 Matacapan, Cerro de las Mesas; 25 Tepeapulco; 26 Laguna Zope

MONTE ALBÁN

The capital of the first state was Monte Albán. Its foundation in about 500 BC, atop a mountain at the junction of the Valley of Oaxaca's three arms, was a spectacular gesture. With the accumulation of more than a thousand years of monuments and its sweeping views across to the surrounding mountains, it is one of the most dramatic archaeological sites in Mexico (plate 8). It is generally agreed that it was the work of the Zapotecs who, by implication, were also the people of the Valley before 500 BC and who remain the region's largest Native group today.

The site was new. Its founding population was about 5000. It rose threefold in four centuries and, by AD 700, it was about 24,000. By the end of the first millennium BC, the top of the mountain was flattened out as a plaza which was then filled and surrounded by ceremonial buildings, and perhaps the governors' houses. Most people occupied terraces built on the surrounding slopes (as at San Lorenzo [chapter 3]). They may have made dams to catch water but must have depended on farms in the Valley below for their food. That demanded massive surplus harvests there.

It is moot as to whether the state created Monte Albán or whether the state formed through the organizational requirements of developing and supporting the town and building power in and around the Valley. The settlement pattern remained comparatively simple for a few generations. San José Mogote and half of the villages between it and Monte Albán were abandoned, presumably as the inhabitants moved to the new capital; but, further afield, Yegüih and two successive sites near San Martín Tilcajete seem to have remained at first, perhaps as independent centres. Prof. Blanton has detected three groups of housing on the mountain in the first phase of occupation and suggests that they were colonies, one from each arm of the surrounding valley. He draws the implication that Monte Albán was a federal project and that the site was selected for geographic neutrality as much as for its magnificence.

Why was Monte Albán founded? Blanton and colleagues have suggested that the Valley was divided, during the previous couple of centuries, between its three arms. Federation may, thus, have been intended to settle local conflict. Or there may have been a threat from beyond. The Valley was surely the most productive district in the region. It was perhaps for peaceable trade, then, but perhaps in defence that, from about 500 BC, settlements developed along routes into the Valley. Among the earliest monuments at Monte Albán was a set of some 300 stone carvings like the one at San José Mogote (chapter 3). Dubbed Danzantes, dancers, they are shown with limbs twisted and eyes shut. Most are decorated with scrolls that may represent gore. The Danzantes are usually interpreted as the corpses of enemy soldiers, whether from beyond the Valley or within. A. A. Joyce, on the other hand, arguing for 'agency' (chapter 1), suggests that Monte Albán was developed first for a cult in response to social and political change (compare chapter 3).

With current estimates of the dating of pottery collected from villages of the time, it looks as though population in the Valley and surrounding districts began to grow quickly. Households at El Palmillo worked busily for centuries at various crafts. Maguey was an important material for them and may have provided food and drink too, since the site is in a dry zone. At Hierve el Agua, irrigation ditches lie fossilized by minerals. Whether on account of competition or of administrative reorganization, villages became more evenly distributed.

In their surveys, Prof. Blanton and colleagues have detected changing proportions of population in Monte Albán itself and secondary centres such as San José Mogote (which was revived). Indeed, by AD 700, Jalieza was as big as Monte Albán and growing. Pottery forms varied with the size and function of settlements; and the quality, diversity and homogeneity of these goods varied from period to period. The archaeologists hold that these variations mark differences and fluctuations in the standard of living and they have sought to correlate them with cycles of administrative control and enterprise, even claiming to have found a large conveniently located market place. Perhaps, then, it was on account of increasing integration – and declining domestic autonomy – that the volume of household storage was diminishing by 300 BC. Not that that necessarily affected social status: one of the richest burials was made not at Monte Albán but in little Santo Domingo Tomaltepec.

The same team has shown that the distribution and extent of the whole settlement pattern fluctuated. Since this instability cannot all be ascribed to changes in climate, they have argued that it was partly the effect of state policy; but it would be interesting to assess soils for evidence of agricultural management or degradation.

Influence from the Valley Zapotecs can be traced among the remains of the Mixtec towns developing in the valleys to the north-west. At Huachino, pottery and architecture look so Zapotec that the site must have been a colony. Monte Negro shows the influence too; but, here and elsewhere, a distinct form of temple was retained; sites such as Etlatongo are defensible; and it can be argued that urban development was a local response to Zapotec aggression. Imitations of the Valley's grey pottery have been found widely in southern Mexico, and the real thing was exported to Cerro de la Cruz and Río Viejo, and as far as Laguna Zope.

Not content with trade during the last couple of centuries BC, the Zapotecs went conquering. At Monte Albán is a series of epigraphic texts which have been provisionally deciphered as records of vanquished communities, analogous, perhaps, to the Danzantes. Not all of the claims are necessarily to be believed but, in the warm Cuicatlán valley, along the route to Tehuacán, there are signs of occupation and exploitation: imported pottery; settlement abruptly shifted off the best soils; perhaps a fort at Quiotepec, a frontier beyond which the Zapotec evidence diminishes; and a set of adults' and children's skulls apparently strung up on racks as did the Aztecs with their victims'. Paradoxically, perhaps, the same period, at home in the Valley, brought declining population.

As for the rulers and their courts, little is known. Stelae and paintings on the walls of tombs at Monte Albán show figures in various costumes and poses. Short texts, found on monuments and in houses at Monte Albán and in tombs at Cuilapan and Lambityeco, may be lists of pedigree. Yet some archaeologists suspect that the reason that kings elude them here is that Monte Albán's was a corporate state.

Some of the tombs at Monte Albán are minor architectural feats, painted extensively, and furnished with a wealth of goods – surely the vaults of nobles. Some of the wall paintings and the elaborate urns which accompanied the dead depict spirits in detail. Most of the principal figures are obviously related to contemporary and later deities known from Central Mexico and among the Maya.

From the later AD 100s, Monte Albán showed influence from Teotihuacan in formal architectural style. A set of stelae depicts figures carrying ritual paraphernalia and wearing ceremonial costumes and Teotihuacano insignia. They appear to be greeted by a Zapotec dignitary. Teotihuacanos are recorded as attending a royal function. There are hints of a military context. Teotihuacan's influence shows in pottery and sculpture in the Mixtec valleys too. Whatever the purpose of these exchanges, a wider view of Mexico shows that Teotihuacan was now the greater power.

CITY OF THE GODS

'Teotihuacan' is a corruption of the Aztec name for the site, 'City of the gods'. The whole scale of the place is profoundly inspiring. It certainly is an archaeologist's paradise (plate 9); but archaeological survey has confirmed that the city's early history was cataclysmic.

Back in 500 BC, there was no reason to anticipate that. Probably on account of higher rainfall, most of the Valley of Mexico's population remained, as a thousand years before, in the south-east. By 100 BC, however, the two principal towns, Cuicuilco and Teotihuacan, were at the edges of the district (15). Both seem to have comprised residential compounds laid out in grid plans – probably a more formal version of the house clusters at Loma Torremote (chapter 3); and Cuicuilco was dominated by a large ceremonial platform. Between these towns, there seems to have been gradual growth and development; but Cuicuilco seems to have begun to draw people in from the villages around it.

Then the scene was shattered by a volcano which buried Cuicuilco in lava and fanned ash across the fertile farms to the east. In a single day, the people of the previous world were drowned, according to the Aztecs' Legend of the Suns, and the sky was hidden. The date of the eruption is in doubt: new research makes it as late as AD 280.

A number of hilltop occupations, dating from about the turn of the millennium, may hint of insecurity closer to Teotihuacan; but then any problems were resolved by progressively drawing nearly the whole population of the Valley of Mexico into Teotihuacan (15). Villages, evenly distributed for almost a thousand years before, had first shifted toward the burgeoning city and then just disappeared. So much for a tiered settlement pattern!

East and south of the old town, two long streets were laid out perpendicular to each other (16). The view along the grander of them, running south–north, shows the Moon Pyramid framed, perhaps with suggestions of productivity (chapter 1), by the curved profile of Cerro Gordo, 'Fat Hill'. Forming a consistent grid plan, all subsequent development respected this axis. There is speculation as to the astronomical significance of the orientation. The 'Great Compound' was left open beside the crossroads (it is now occupied

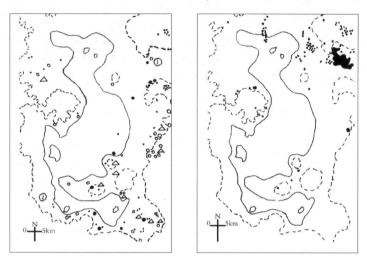

15 The rise of Teotihuacan, from (left map) about 100 BC to (right map) first
century AD (after Sanders et al. 1979). The continuous line marks the lake edge,
the broken line the foot of the mountains. Triangles mark small towns, filled
circles larger villages, empty circles smaller villages, and dots hamlets. On the left
map, 1 marks Teotihuacan, 2 Cuicuilco

by facilities for tourism). In the first, second and third centuries
AD, the two great pyramids were built in phases, first the earlier
stages of the Sun and Moon Pyramids, and then, soon after 200, the
Feathered Serpent or Quetzalcoatl pyramid in the plaza known as
the Citadel. Visitors can find traces of the paint on these monuments
that would have caught the eye from afar.

The population reached about 70–100,000 by AD 100 and doubled during the next two centuries. As extensive as Rome at the
same time, it became one of the world's half-dozen biggest cities.

Whether or not the city's cult attracted the newcomers, the
prior laying out of the principal streets implies that policy led
the way. South of the Sun Pyramid, the principal street was inter-
rupted, in about AD 300, by an enclosure that some archaeologists
interpret as a precinct for the governors. G.L. Cowgill surmises
that they were oligarchs relying for popular compliance on pro-
motion of moral discipline and ideology. No doubt they made
use of spectacular ceremonies among the monuments, but Prof.

Cowgill suspects that the dedication of the Feathered Serpent temple prompted a shift of policy. Either for the temple itself or for the sake of the person or persons presumably buried in one of the two central vaults – looted long before the archaeologists reached it – were buried nearly 200 people, including splendidly outfitted soldiers with votive goods. Many lay with their arms apparently tied behind the back. Some decades later, the building was wrecked and a new platform built over its facade. It was at about this time that the new precinct was laid out. Does it imply a new order, less dependent on processions among the monuments, more centralized, perhaps? Indeed, other than enhancements of existing ones, no major monuments were built thereafter; but the stock of housing compounds increased. Was this a response to popular revulsion against mass sacrifice; or did it relate to the disaster at Cuicuilco?

Sacrifice did continue. Recent investigations of the Moon Pyramid revealed five tombs. In one, the bodies' posture and lavish burial goods were reminiscent of Maya interments (see chapter 5). Another held ten beheaded corpses accompanying a pair richly adorned; and this one included pumas, wolves, eagles and an owl. It was made in the 200s as part of an enhancement of the pyramid. One was the tomb of a puma. Later Mesoamericans would have associated the cats with the underworld or night-time Sun, the eagles with the sky or day-time Sun, and the people as just people, sacrifices, that is, for maintaining life, keeping the Sun in circulation around us (34).

In the present state of research, though, we can but speculate. There is a Teotihuacano style of sculpture, wall paintings and pottery. The architecture is distinguished by the 'talud & tablero' (batter & fascia; plate 10), a motif anticipated a little earlier at Tetimpa, in the Puebla basin, to the east, where house groups lie preserved under volcanic ash with their granaries, fields and irrigation channels. Some of the religious symbols may derive from the same region, including the arrangement of domestic temples, while wall paintings and pottery are reminiscent of designs developed earlier on the Gulf Coast. Yet the best clues must lie among the ruins themselves. They were surveyed more than 30 years ago, and, along

with selective digs, study of the results continues. The main foci
have been religion, social relations and industry.

CITY LIFE

The Aztecs' curiosity about Teotihuacan may have revealed ancient
sculptures or even wall paintings that looked familiar to them:
the Feathered Serpent, for instance, or the images of a blood-
thirsty eagle emerging from a seashell, and of the jaguar, all corresponding to major cosmic symbols of their own and evidently
the Olmecs too (plate 11). There has been speculation about the
pervasive image of a 'goddess' (plate 12): Prof. Cowgill considers
that it pertains to rulership, but religion was probably an idiom
for many aspects of public life. Yet, unlike the humanistic art of
the Olmecs, the Maya or the Aztecs, Teotihuacan's style is of masks
and geometry.

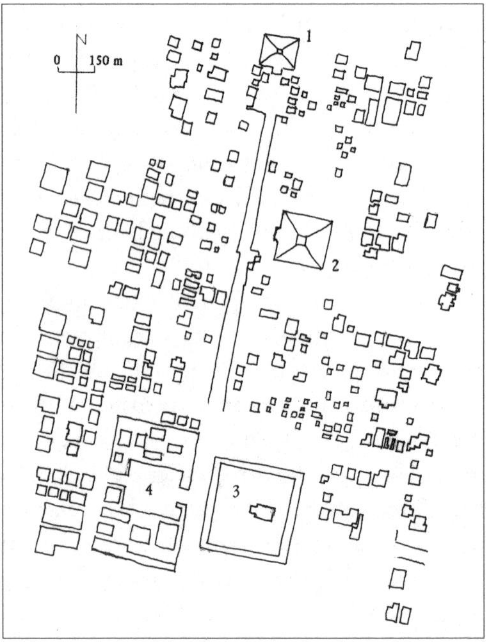

16 Teotihuacan:
sketch plan of
the central zone,
marking 1 Pyramid
of the Moon, 2
Pyramid of the
Sun, 3 'Citadel'
& Quetzalcoatl
Pyramid, 4 the Great
Compound; note
the many domestic
compounds

The three largest pyramids would have supported temples; other shrines lined the way from the Pyramid of the Moon and were distributed throughout the city. Yet, for all the splendid layout and architecture, and its vivid art, the city seems impersonal, airless. A tour among the residential quarters can help to explain this paradox.

A few thousand people lived in comparatively flimsy houses but, by about 350, the great majority occupied soundly built compounds, up to a hundred people together. Some 2200 compounds have been found. Density varied; some were very commodious. The quality of building and decoration varied too. Bones from one of the plainer and less substantial compounds and from modest houses have yielded 'rich' burials. We do not know whether the city was divided by social strata or if affluence varied along a continuum. It is thought that the governors may have lived beside the Quetzalcoatl pyramid.

There may have been groups of compounds for populations from a couple of hundred up to about 3000. Wealthier residents may have lived in the middle of these neighbourhoods. Walls up to 5m high divided parts of the city. The grandest houses tend to cluster near the north end of the main street. Debris of potting and obsidian knapping have revealed industrial zones. Yet few of these distinctions are clear.

The basic unit was the compound, then, rather than the neighbourhood – the city does not look conducive to gossip! Access to compounds was restricted by circuit walls; and many (or all) maintained their own shrines (plate 13). At least some compounds had wells within. On the other hand, excavation of one richly appointed site found little or no evidence for making flour, so that the inhabitants may have depended on outsiders for this basic task. Compounds were long lived, some rebuilt three or four times over. One sample of bones, with which hereditary conditions were studied, implies that men remained in the compound where they were born and obtained wives from others; but one case where women seem to have stayed put has been found too. Perhaps the compounds' exclusivity reflects initial immigration from different parts of the Valley of Mexico.

How, then, did Teotihuacan work? Of its governors, more, if anything, is known from inscriptions at Monte Albán and among the Maya than in the city itself. As with Monte Albán, authority is thought to have been 'corporate', perhaps theocratic. Some archaeologists read the triple tasselled headdress shown in later art, and in pictures of Teotihuacano visitors at Monte Albán and among the Maya, as a sign of authority.

The grid plan is the city's most basic symbol. Saburo Sugiyama has argued that the distribution and proportions of the main structures along the north–south axial street were worked out in reference to calendrical arithmetic, notably the cycle of 260 days (chapter 1). There are hints in wall paintings of the Ball Game and a kind of lacrosse, but courts have not been found. Prof. Cowgill suspects that the government sought to regulate more of religious life than just municipal rites: certain vessels of standardized forms that may have been used in worship at home were made near buildings probably associated with the governors. They fell out of use once the city declined. Cowgill also suggests that iconography in various media indicates certain military corps recruited across lines of local or family loyalty. Alfredo & Leonardo López (historian father and archaeologist son) consider that the cult of the Feathered Serpent was later exploited elsewhere, with military connotations, to symbolize authority among heterogeneous societies. Did Teotihuacan create the prototype in order to gather its diverse communities?

Not the least puzzle is lack of writing. It now seems that there was a system of notation but, unlike Zapotec, Maya and later scripts, it was not linear.

How much complementary economic specialization was there or how self-sufficient were the compounds? It is thought that as many as a third of Teotihuacanos worked in manufacturing and services. There seem to have been hundreds of workshops, including scores of potteries and stone knapping sites. That some were near temples or grander housing suggests institutional control. Teotihuacan probably controlled the district's obsidian quarries but, without painstaking examination, it is not easy to distinguish industrial debris from rubbish tips. Since most people probably lived barefooted, it was important to tidy up chips of obsidian. Did specialists work full-time?

For every person not engaged in producing food, another had to harvest a surplus. The ancient skills of fishing, fowling and snaring flourished but the city cannot have depended on them. Where, then, were the fields? Some countryside was repopulated but, failing alternative sources of power for transport, there must have been highly intensive farms near the city. There were concentrations of hamlets around the city. The western ones may possibly have practised intensive lakeside cultivation (*15*; see chapter 7); and there are traces of this technique within the city limits. There are traces of irrigation too. The land south of the city has long been irrigated and it is commonly assumed that this must have been Teotihuacan's bread basket. If that was so, then the requirements of co-ordinating labour there could help to explain the development of government in the city; but, of all Teotihuacan's secrets, its farms are the most basic.

How were food and manufactures distributed? There is a spread of jars that suggests storage; and the Great Compound is commonly interpreted as a market place but, again, that begs questions! Nor is the supply and drainage of domestic water understood; although they were canalized, some streams and a small river seem hardly adequate; three tanks and a small reservoir have been identified.

TEOTIHUACHAN ABROAD

Not all of the city's requirements could be met locally. The recent discovery of a pyramid nearly 50 km to the south shows that some outlying communities were substantial. If further parts of the Valley of Mexico were used for nothing else, at least the need for firewood must have drawn collectors out. Other resources had to be brought from further afield. Growth of population at and around Chingú may have been to quarry lime for Teotihuacan's buildings and its kitchens (nixtamal). Like the capital, the town was laid out in a grid and people lived in compounds. Most of the obsidian too came from neighbouring districts. The pattern of sources and the form of tools at Tepeapulco indicate industrialization at the cost of workshops elsewhere in the area. Settlement was concentrated and the town provided with its own pyramid.

Some archaeologists suspect that export of the green obsidian from Pachuca, in the same district, to all parts of Mesomerica was the secret of Teotihuacan's success. The city's distinctive Thin Orange pottery too turns up throughout Mesoamerica, including a ribbon of sites along the route through the Puebla basin to the east, the 'Teotihuacan corridor'.

In Morelos, there is evidence for a venture like the Zapotec conquest of the Cuicatlán valley. Finds of pottery suggest that Cuicuilco had had interest in the region. This material was succeeded by locally made wares in Teotihuacano style, including tripod vessels and Thin Orange. The settlement pattern changed, with hamlets dispersed in a zone of high water table and a large new centre at San Ignacio. Just as the Zapotecs may have concentrated on crops that would not grow in their higher Valley, so may Teotihuacan in Morelos. The best guess is that cotton was what they wanted – one of the main commodities later to interest the Aztecs here. Tellingly, as Teotihuacan waned, the settlement pattern reverted.

More even-handed relations may have prevailed with the Zapotecs. Not only are Teotihuacanos recorded at Monte Albán but also there is a group of compounds in west Teotihuacan with pottery in the Zapotec style of the same period (or slightly earlier) and burial vaults in the Zapotec manner. Other finds suggest that the immigrants were plasterers, and, indeed, similar pottery has been found at Chingú. Further finds in the same part of the city suggest a colony from western Mexico.

In northeast Teotihuacan, there are compounds with both pottery and buildings in the style of the Gulf Coast and lowland Maya pottery too. Perhaps the 'Maya' burial in the Moon Pyramid honoured a colony. Teotihuacanos returned these visits during the fifth and sixth centuries. Signs of their influence are clear at and around El Tajín, at Matacapan, and, mingling with late Olmec tradition and elements from Oaxaca and the Maya, at Cerro de las Mesas. A field system in the same region has been tentatively ascribed to surveyors influenced by Teotihuacan. Teotihuacan may have had catalytic political effects among the lowland Maya too (see next chapter). However, its presence looks stronger among the highlanders, at Kaminaljuyu.

Teotihuacan's influence is found to the north as well and far to the north-west, at Alta Vista, where there were mines for copper ores, cinnabar and greenstone (crysacola). Increased rainfall, part of a worldwide climatic fluctuation, seems to have favoured more farming in the region between about AD 150 and 500. Macaw feathers and iron ore mirrors in southern Arizona show that, directly or probably indirectly, Mexico reached much further afield too.

Between its furthest reaches and the inner zone sprang up a band of places where Teotihuacan's influence mingled with others'. Teotihuacan's development was reflected at Cholula, which went on to flourish from 400 to the seventh century, with stelae and altars in Gulf Coast fashion from Oaxaca, before apparently decaying in about 700. Xochicalco, refounded, in effect, in the later seventh century, seems to display affinities with Teotihuacan as well as other regions. Other places, however, seem less receptive to the metropolis (chapter 6).

THE PIVOT OF MESOAMERICAN HISTORY?

What was the nature of Teotihuacan's influence, then? In order to assess the two principal theories, a summary is needed, first, of its history and geography.

Beyond the Valley of Mexico, Teotihuacan's influence tended to grow from the later 200s, corresponding, perhaps, to the apparent changes in municipal policy on monuments, and perhaps too to the iconography of militarism. Some archaeologists detect a distinct phase of history corresponding to Teotihuacan's ascendancy abroad. Certainly, the city's influence waned after about 250 years. The decline may have been an economic effect of the reversal of the earlier climatic improvement (for which there is other evidence from Europe and China). A fundamental and inadequately acknowledged technical problem is that the city's later history and eventual fall remain to be securely dated.

Other than the Valley of Mexico, only in Morelos is Teotihuacano material clearly related to changes in settlement pattern. Strong influence on formal architecture in Kaminaljuyu probably indicates a more limited presence. Elsewhere, the influence seems to have been just in particular features of architecture or crafts while, on Monte Albán, imports were restricted to the quarters of the elite.

The usual interpretation of Teotihuacan's presence in so many regions is that the city depended on them for commodities – cotton from Morelos, for example, or cacao from south of Kaminaljuyu. The suggestion is, then – with the ecological interpretation of Mesoamerican history (chapter 1) – that either, like the Aztecs, Teotihuacan bound other regions into tributary relations or it traded for imports with products of its own.

The other approach is more a political one. There are two versions of it, push and pull. The first suggests that, much like the Aztecs again and perhaps, indeed, in the interest of steady import of critical commodities, Teotihuacan imposed tributary relationships. As with the Aztecs, its requirements may have been symbolic or prestige goods, such as feathers or cacao. According to the pull theory, it was less Teotihuacan that demanded access to other regions than that the latter sought to cultivate relations with the metropolis.

As with the Olmecs, the pull theory begs fewer questions and makes the most sense of variations in the local evidence. The growth witnessed in so many parts of Mesoamerica at the time will have engendered local needs for an idiom of power and prestige. As with the Olmecs, it would have been less that Teotihuacan offered a new message than that its art style encoded familiar principles in a compelling way. Esther Pasztory has suggested that, partly by virtue of standardization and modularity, the style permitted clear and idealized, abstract presentation of symbols. In this view, Teotihuacan's idiom was taken up variously in one district and another. Exchange with the metropolis would have been in the hands of elites, with few direct consequences for their followers. Yet the push theory may account better for later events in Teotihuacan itself (chapter 6).

It is exciting to study the big monuments – and public funders concerned with economic development know that tourists agree – but if more energy were devoted to studying ordinary everyday life, Teotihuacan's impacts on Mesoamerica would look less pervasive. The notion of a 'golden age' haunted later history; but did it refer to Teotihuacan in particular; and was it merely the lore of aristocrats?

THE WEST

Western Mexico was something of a world unto itself from about 1000 BC. It has long been renowned for superbly moulded and painted pottery figures dating from about 500 BC and perhaps throughout the Classic period (plate 14). They appear to illustrate a great range of activity from domestic life – replete with succulent dogs – to rites, including the Ball Game and the 'flier' ceremony in which, attached by cords, performers swing from the top of a pole. However, by analogy with modern rites of the Huichols, P.T. Furst has argued that much of this art illustrates beliefs about afterlife. Most of the figures do come from tombs but nearly all were looted without record. Only now are the fruits of systematic fieldwork providing a coherent context for them.

By 300 BC, graves in the district around Tequila, and in the Bolaños drainage to the north, were placed at the bottom of shafts marked by mounds (the National Museum of Anthropology, Mexico City, displays a reconstruction). This rite may have been developed from sunken tombs of the type dug a thousand years earlier at El Opeño or, again, it may have been influenced from north-western South America (chapter 3). Many or most of the shafts are barely 2m deep but one tomb at Huitzilapa was 8m deep and one at El Arenal all of 18m! Both of the latter sites had three shafts, each leading to a couple of vaults containing several bodies. Tombs of this type were commonly surrounded by a ring of little buildings at ground level and by other structures including, in some cases if not all, ball courts. Of six bodies in one of the vaults at Huitzilapa, five shared a common deformity of the spine, which suggests that they were of a single family. The distinction between the majority of more modest tombs and the elaborate ones with ancillary buildings suggests a hierarchy of sites; and the osteology at Huitzilapa suggests a chiefly dynasty.

From about AD 300, the grander tombs in the Teuchitlán area were less elaborate but more buildings accompanied them, giving rise to circles of pavilions. The figurines accompanying the burials look more formal, but pottery models illustrated various activities – at least one shows a lively assembly around a shaft grave. Although population may have been rising, parts of the countryside were deserted and the main sites grew, giving rise to perhaps four tiers of settlement. P.C. Weigand has found evidence for intensively maintained wetland fields in the same period; and he has also identified defensive sites around the edges of the district and, beyond, outlying sites which he interprets as colonies for supplying the central district. On the other hand, although Cerro del Agua Escondida and its neighbours are thought to have supplied the Teuchitlán district with salt during the dry season, settlement here remained uncentralized, as though this area was autonomous.

The pattern and process of development in the Teuchitlán district is reminiscent of Teotihuacan but there is no direct evidence of the city's influence. That shows elsewhere in the region, at El Ixtépete, Tingambato and La Campana and, to the north, La Quemada and perhaps Alta Vista, with batter & fascia and, or, pottery and figurines.

5

The ancient Maya

The ancient Maya, the ruins of pyramid-studded cities abandoned to the forests, their art, mathematics and astronomy, have long fascinated and mystified us. Thanks to a great deal of new excavation and survey and long strides in deciphering their writing, much of the mystery is giving way to specific questions about social and political organization and technology; but it will be many years more before they are cleared up.

From the earlier first millennium BC, the style of art, crafts and architecture herald a story which can be traced up to today. Yet it is marked by two major crises: the 'collapse' of Classic Maya civilization in the ninth century, and the Spanish Conquest. The present chapter covers the 16 or 17 centuries to the eve of the collapse, the greater parts of the Formative and Classic periods (5). First, it traces the history of the principal urban centres, and then it sketches out the main features of daily life during the Classic (17).

FIRST PYRAMIDS

Although small populations had long inhabited the southern mountains and Yucatan, most prehistorians consider that Maya history begins with colonization of the central region from the coasts. The people of the Gulf and Pacific coasts are thought to have been related, on account partly of the 'Xe' style of pottery common to both and partly of the modern distribution of the Mixean languages (2). On grounds of pottery style, the Caribbean pioneers are assumed to have descended from the Pacific population.

In the earlier part of the first millennium BC, growing populations along the Pacific coast began to settle inland. The number of villages increased and eventually filled back toward the coast. Several boasted sculptures or carvings of chiefs or, perhaps, their ancestors – reminiscent of the early figurines in the region and of the Olmecs. The biggest site, Izapa, comprises about 3km^2 of consistently oriented plazas and mounds. In the later part of the millennium, stelae were put up, many with stones set before them like altars. Many of the stelae depict elaborately garbed people and other creatures. Features of the style and much of the iconography – Earth, underworld and Sky, and the Tree that links them – prefigure later art; and there are figures recognizable from later versions, in cities to the north, as the spirit of rain and lightning and the snake-footed patron of royalty.

In the highlands, the small cemetery of Los Mangales covered a series of house platforms dating from the earlier first millennium BC. On one of them was a fixed bench containing a burial – later a common form. It was a man's, with, among other goods, three severed heads; and around it were at least a dozen other burials. The pattern is similar to Monument 22 at Chalcatzingo, roughly contemporary (chapter 3). Like the hall at Paso de la Amada, the grave may have represented a leading dynasty. During the following centuries, the district's population grew and a new ceremonial site was developed at El Portón, with a series of stelae and altars. One stela is carved with glyphs – from about 400 BC, probably the earliest known Maya text.

Similar developments took place on a grander scale at Kaminaljuyu. By 300 BC, it was bigger than Izapa. There were stelae like the ones at Izapa, some with texts yet undeciphered. Kaminaljuyu was dominated by groups of mounds or platforms, some 200 in all. Some of the mounds contained burials. In any one period, one of these tombs was evidently preeminent. The best known mound included two successive interments accompanied by the bodies of retainers and a wealth of pottery and ritual paraphernalia. Here too, then, dynastic cults may have been fostered in order to legitimate new powers, possibly over irrigation, remains of which have been discovered, or over the obsidian quarries 20km away at El Chayal, perhaps an asset for trade.

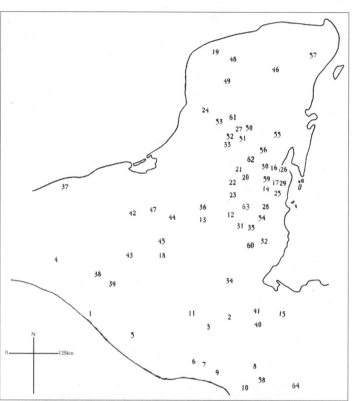

17 The ancient Maya: 1 Izapa; 2 Los Mangales; 3 Kaminaljuyu; 4 Chiapa de Corzo; 5 Abaj Tak'alik'; 6 El Baúl; 7 Bilbao; 8 Chalchuapa; 9 Monte Alto; 10 Santa Leticia; 11 La Lagunita; 12 Tik'al; 13 Altar de Sacrificios; 14 Cuello; 15 Los Higos; 16 Dos Hombres, La Milpa; 17 K'axob; 18 Bonampak; 19 Komchen, Tz'ibilchaltun; 20 Nak'be, San Bartolo; 21 El Mirador; 22 Wakna; 23 Waxaktun; 24 Etz'na; 25 Lamanai; 26 Cerros; 27 Bekan; 28 Kahal Pech; 29 Kolha; 30 Nohmul; 31 Yaxha; 32 Caracol; 33 Kalak'mul; 34 Kankuwen; 35 Naranjo; 36 El Perú; 37 Comalcalco; 38 Chinkultic; 39 Tenam Rosario; 40 Copan; 41 Quirigua; 42 Palenque; 43 Tonina; 44 Piedras Negras; 45 Yaxchilan; 46 Yaxuna; 47 Pomona; 48 Akankeh; 49 Oxk'intok'; 50 Xpuhil; 51 Río Bec; 52 Chikanna; 53 Hochob; 54 Barton Ramie; 55 Dzibanche; 56 Kohunlich; 57 Koba; 58 Cerén; 59 Pulltrouser Swamp; 60 Dos Pilas; 61 Balamku; 62 Río Azul; 63, Holmul, Cival; 64 Quelepa

By the end of the millennium, it is thought, trade was a main-stay at Chiapa de Corzo, Abaj Tak'alik', El Baúl, and Chalchuapa too (17). Usulatan style pottery is found throughout, there are similarities among stelae, and a type of 'pot belly' sculpture is found at all four places, at Kaminaljuyu and, famously, at Monte Alto and Santa Leticia – recall again the plump figurines long before in Soconusco. Sculpture at La Lagunita and elsewhere among the mountains to the north shows affinities with Izapa and Kaminaljuyu.

Yet, except, on present evidence, at La Lagunita, it all stopped in the earlier part of the fifth century AD. No more stelae were put up. Kaminaljuyu and the other larger places declined. Many sites were completely abandoned. The disruption is attributed to the volcano Ilopango which burst near San Salvador, showering ash over the landscape. The region would not revive for centuries.

Population had been growing along the southern Caribbean as well and, partly, no doubt, for that reason but partly too, perhaps, on account of rising sea level, settlers moved upriver by the later second millennium BC. Others may have converged on the central lowlands along the western waterways too while yet other colonists moved in from the highlands.

By about 700 BC, there were three hamlets at Tik'al. At K'axob, within a couple of centuries more, a larger house was distinguished from its neighbours by increasingly elaborate burial rites. Some settlements were dignified with platforms for public rites. The one at Altar de Sacrificios stood 4m above a plaza. Rebuilding at Cuello, in the fifth century, was marked by burying two dozen young people – at least some of them hacked up. At La Milpa and Dos Hombres, villagers from the vicinity laid out ceremonial mounds, plazas and ball courts late in the first millennium. Radiating from Etz'na, 22km of canals evince mass labour; and, at Yaxuna, a very large platform dates from the same period.

The story makes sense, by analogy with the south, as progressive elaboration of political and ritual organization; but discoveries in the Peten have shown that either some chapters are still missing and, or, the process was not always gradual. At Nak'be, in about 700 BC, a massive platform was built with a pyramid standing on it

18 Masks on an early pyramid at Piedras Negras. Note the stelae (compare plate 16)

as high as 18m. A couple of centuries later, much bigger pyramids were built, decorated with huge plaster faces and crowned with three shrines, a pattern known as a triadic structure. Another pattern – an 'E-Group' – comprised a pyramid with a long mound facing it across a plaza from the east. Some of these complexes were linked by causeways (sakbes, 'white roads' of limestone). By 300 BC, similar buildings, and also stelae, were put up at El Mirador. This place was the grandest of them all: the central ceremonial zone spreads across 2km²; crowned wih a triadic structure, the Tigre pyramid rose 55m, while the Danta pyramid exploited a hillock to reach 70m! A causeway runs the 14km to Nak'be, Wakna (Güiro) and Tintal, in the same district. Further afield, Tik'al and Waxaktun, Etz'na, Lamanai and Cerros were provided with like buildings and decor. The most elaborate plaster decorations found are Balamku's, which appear to date from the third century AD. Some three centuries earlier is the mural, recently discovered at San Bartolo, apparently depicting a royal offering of food to a god of corn; and shown too seems to be a Feathered Serpent. Some of this iconography, in turn, may compare to plasterwork, found at Cival, dated to the second century BC, which includes resemblances to Olmec motifs.

What did these buildings and their ornament mean? By analogy with later iconography, the masks are thought to represent spirits, notably the Sun and Venus, and Earth, the 'sacred mountain' of origin and fertility. At Cerros, if not elsewhere, they may represent governors too. E-groups may have been designed to mark solstices and equinoxes. Thus, rites, dances and processions among these buildings would have connoted both cosmic and political power. Yet Cerros is enclosed by a ditch or moat – water storage, sacred boundary or defence? Bekan was enclosed, in about the third century AD, by a both a moat and a clearly defensive rampart.

Whether by dint of force or by virtue of deference, it was an increasingly hierarchical society. Elaborate tombs were set among ceremonial buildings at Wakna and Tik'al. Forest hinders survey in most of the region but it looks as though Tik'al and Waxaktun were related as capital and satellite. There were probably similar constellations to the east. El Mirador's size and its array of cause-ways suggest a very extensive domain. El Mirador's were, indeed, the most massive monuments in Maya history; but, although, like the Olmec centres, they could have been the focus of some grand cult, El Mirador was not necessarily the capital of a state.

Here again, development is thought to have been stimulated by trade. Exchange along the Caribbean could have encouraged northward colonization in the first place; and then requirements of salt and stone implements inland may have stimulated trade to the communities growing there. Remains of seafood have been found at Kahal Pech and as far inland as Tik'al. The people of Kolha evidently quarried and worked chert for tools; Komchen may have specialized in trading salt. Usulutan ware was brought to El Mirador and Tik'al, and, at the latter, a small 'pot bellied' sculpture has been found.

Yet El Mirador, Nak'be, Cerros and others failed during the later second century. At La Milpa, erosion implies that farmers had not allowed enough fallow; and soil at El Mirador and Nak'be indicates drought. Tik'al and Waxaktun, on the other hand, lived on to greater things. Decline of the route along the south may have allowed them to develop a portage between the Caribbean and the Gulf of Mexico.

The pattern of evidence corresponds to the principles recognised for Teotihuacan or Monte Albán as the archaeology of 'the state'; and, as there, so too the first Maya rulers remain unknown, perhaps because authority was 'corporate' (chapter 1). More research is needed, however: for example, the evidence of the causeways is not necessarily consistent; but, more broadly, until politics and 'power', and their 'meanings', are better understood for the early Maya, interpretation will remain blunt. Decipherment of the texts from the succeeding period reveals local relations (and 'agency') more complicated than strictly archaeological criteria could anticipate.

ALLIES AND RIVALS

From the third century AD to the early tenth, the Classic period, much of Maya life centred around several groups of cities and towns whose rulers drew tribute from satellite communities. Much more is known, for this period, about royal courts, thanks to inscriptions on stone (plate 15). It is as though, unlike Teotihuacan or Monte Albán, the Maya now adopted the 'network' strategy centred on the power of the kings (chapter 1). For the first part of the period, one of the key issues is Teotihuacan's role in the political development of the regional capitals: was it encouraging an international 'network'; or was it more that Maya courts adopted and adapted Teotihuacan's corporate idiom for their own ambitions?

The third century witnessed redevelopment in the eastern lowlands. Population rose; the village at Barton Ramie doubled in size. More Usulutan ware was introduced. Development at Nohmul, even while Cerros, in the same district, failed, suggests that immigrants upset the balance and created a new order. Perhaps a similar process allowed Tik'al to dominate the Mirador district. Two of Tik'al's earliest aristocratic tombs were decorated with paintings in southern style.

Tik'al eventually covered more than 30km^2, with at least 60,000 inhabitants (_19_). Building tended to respect a common orientation but both density and distribution of housing were quite unlike

Teotihuacan's. About 11,000 are thought to have lived in the central zone, including 3000 in palaces; and survey suggests that another 30,000 lived in hamlets around the city. Most archaeological attention has been devoted to the centre, which was dominated by temples on soaring pyramids (plate 16).

Later inscriptions imply that the rise of Tik'al owed to Yax Ehb' Xok (First Step Shark), credited with founding the royal dynasty in about AD 90. Records of successors, here and in other towns, provide a framework for Tik'al's remaining history. In 378 'arrived' First Crocodile and Fire-Born (or Fire Is Born; known until recent revisions as Curl Nose and Smoking Frog, respectively). Fire-Born was previously recorded at El Perú (Waka') to the west; and at Tik'al he was also titled Lord of the West. Other carvings (including the image of the tasselled headdress – see p.66) and associated architectural features, pottery and tombs (one of them probably that of 'Stormy Sky', First Crocodile's son and successor) imply – or were meant to imply – that these men were Teotihuacano. Finds of pottery and the green obsidian from Pachuca confirm the connection. At the satellite town of Yaxha, a stela shows the headdress again. Wall painting in an aristocratic precinct at Holmul shows armed Teotihuacanos with Maya kitted out for the Ball Game; and here too were found pottery in Teotihuacano style and green obsidian. These finds have now been dated by radiocarbon to AD 377. Whether by force – as one group burial suggests – or by diplomatic marriage, Fire-Born soon took power at Waxaktun as well. At Río Azul, inscriptions and a set of carvings that depict executions of nobles suggest that Tik'al took over there too a few years later; rapid expansion ensued.

The following generations brought Tik'al into escalating conflict, especially with Kalak'mul and Caracol, both of Tik'al's size. Once linked by causeways to El Mirador and Nak'be, Kalak'mul was dominated by a platform and triadic structure of the ancient type. Around the ceremonial precinct, along the western slopes of the central zone, and in some suburbs, housing looks denser than in Tik'al. There has been much less digging but Kalak'mul is noted for its many stelae, more than a hundred of them (many, unfortunately, weathered or otherwise illegible). Eventually claim-

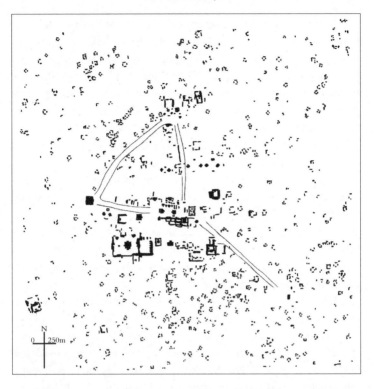

19 Tik'al: the centre and inner suburbs, Temple IV at left centre

ing suzerainty over towns as far as El Perú, Naranjo and even Kankuwen, Kalak'mul was perhaps most formidable of all the Classic powers.

Some prehistorians suspect that Tik'al's conflict with Kalak'mul and Caracol was over long distance trade or possibly over the town of Naranjo (*17*). Others consider that the troubles only became serious as climate cooled in the mid and later sixth century (compare chapter 4). In 556, three years after presiding over a coronation there, Tik'al launched a vicious attack on Caracol – 'axe war', they called it. Six years later, Caracol caught and probably sacrificed the king of Tik'al and pillaged the city. Tik'al's growth ceased, even though many families moved closer in; funerary opulence diminished. Activity declined at and around Río Azul and La Milpa too (although this may have begun before 556). Caracol, on the other hand, burgeoned, becoming about as large as Tik'al. Its inscriptions record attacks on Naranjo in 626, 631 and 636, and it built a stairway there to mark victory. Then Caracol, it seems, was defeated by Naranjo; but, later, it claimed to have captured the king of Tik'al again. At Naranjo, in turn, Lady Six Celestial Lord arrived, in 682, from the aggressive court of Dos Pilas. Naranjo then attacked Ukanal, near Caracol, and dismantled the ignominious stairway, lugging at least one piece of it off to Ukanal!

After further vicissitude, inflicted from Kalak'mul and Dos Pilas, Tik'al revived too, under Hasaw Chan K'awil (Heavenly Standard Bearer; also called Ah Kakaw). When, in 695, he launched an attack on Kalak'mul and captured, among others, the king, Tik'al's supremacy was restored. The city expanded to its greatest extent (plate 16); and resettlement in and around Río Azul suggests restoration of Tik'al's sway there.

Meanwhile, the south had recovered. Linguistic evidence suggests that there may have been immigration from the north. Kaminaljuyu had evidently regained some of its standing by the 300s. In one quarter, from the early fifth century, buildings were remodelled in a local version of Teotihuacano style. By 500, there was major construction in the style, replete with batter & fascia. Burial rites included a seated posture for the corpse used for those burials with Maya goods in Teotihuacan's Moon Pyramid; the bone chemistry here suggests that the dead were local. Amongst the accompanying pottery were Thin Orange ware and increasing amounts of Teotihuacano forms and pieces with typical motifs; and, in the lowlands to the south, caches of Teotihuacano pottery have been found. However, these influences faded during the later 500s.

By analogy with later Aztec interference, some prehistorians consider that Teotihuacan used Kaminaljuyu to control access to the resources of the region. As well as its obsidian, and jade from the Motagua valley, which have been found to the north, Teotihuacan may have been interested in the Pacific district's cacao; and, if this crop succumbed to the cooler weather of the mid 500s, that could help to account for the decline of Teotihuacan's influence. On the other hand, that the crockery did not comprise the whole Teotihuacano service shows that it was not necessarily immigration that explains the evidence. The waxing and waning of Teotihuacano evidence is akin to a 'bell curve' of fashion.

Occupations from the same period are known at several other places in the south, including older ones, such as La Lagunita, Bilbao and Abaj Taka'lik'. By the 600s, the western highlands were densely settled with hamlets and ceremonial centres, greater and smaller, such as Chinkultic and Tenam Rosario.

Best known of the southern cities is Copan. Even here, in the far east, Teotihuacan's 'influence' shows; and there may be an analogy with Teotihuacan's history too. Although long settled, it was not until the early first millennium AD that population grew. There were large ceremonial buildings by about 400. The pottery is reminiscent of Kaminaljuyu. While inscriptions hint at earlier events and rulers, the royal dynasty is always traced back to Yax Kuk Mo, First Quetzal Macaw, who came to power in 426 – perhaps amidst a refugee crisis caused by Ilopango's eruption to the south. Like Fire-Born of Tik'al, he was described as a warrior and as Lord of the West. It may be his bones that were found with goods in Teotihuacano style buried in a platform with batter & fascia beneath the 'acropolis'; but the dental chemistry reveals that this man was probably from the Peten. In another tomb, both the accompanying goods and the corpse's seated posture are reminiscent of Kaminaljuyu.

Copan's population doubled during the mid first millennium, reaching perhaps 10,000 by the seventh century, with another 10,000 in the outskirts, including the site of the modern village. A causeway linked some of the suburbs to the central plaza. Villages and homesteads sprang up elsewhere along the valley as well.

These developments rippled much further afield. Copan's ruler was mentioned at Caracol. Inscriptions on the tall stelae at Quirigua may imply that Copan usurped Tik'al's influence there in the late fifth century, perhaps to extort surplus food. One inscription suggests that Los Higos too was ruled from Copan; and, later, epigraphy, calligraphy, architectural ornaments and pottery show Copan's influence two days' walk to the east.

Prime in the west was lovely Palenque. Although founded about AD 200, at least a century passed before it grew by drawing surrounding villagers in; and its monuments only document royal history from 431. Here too is the mark of Teotihuacan; but it was not until about 600 that the town grew more, to some 7500 inhabitants, partly again, it seems, by pulling people in from surrounding hamlets and, conversely, regulating farm labour. In town, aqueducts and drains were laid out both in the centre and for the middling order of houses in the suburbs.

The longest reign seems to have been King Pakal's (615-83) and it is then that Palenque first finds mention elsewhere. It was then too that the palace, in the middle, took the form now familiar (plate 17; but the tower, unique among the ancient Maya, was added later). The principal pyramids are Pakal's mausoleum and the Cross Group commissioned by his son.

In the hills beyond, rises Tonina on a series of grand terraces. Below lie ball courts. Much of the distinctive sculpture here treats of the game and its association with sacrifice and with war – Palenque was to be reminded about that later (chapter 6). There were several towns along the Usumacinta valley too. Rivals, Piedras Negras and Yaxchilan seem to have grown by drawing people from their respective districts. Piedras Negras became the bigger but inscriptions suggest that Yaxchilan was the most powerful.

In the north, the period is not well understood yet, partly because inscriptions are comparatively scarce here. The best known archaeology are the buildings in Puuk style, many centuries later. While Carmen Varela, studying Oxk'intok', considers that exchange with the south provided the political context for developing the style, others argue for western influence in the ornament. Certainly, Teotihuacano style was accepted in both architecture – at Akankeh, for example, or, for that matter, details at Oxk'intok' – and pottery.

Another style distinguished the middle of the Yucatan peninsula by about AD 500. At Bekan, Xpuhil or Río Bec, temples were built with towers, apparently imitating the grander cities, while, at Chikanna or Hochob, towers were dispensed with but, exploiting the strong sunlight and shadow, the stone facades ornamented in intense detail (Chenes style). Both varieties feature symbols of the sacred mountain and other signs known from contemporary and earlier monuments in the central area. To the east too, there were affinities with the central area from about AD 250–600. Digs at Dzibanche and Kohunlich, respectively, have revealed the ancient triadic pattern of shrines and temples decorated with faces of the spirit of time or the Sun.

The biggest city in the north was Koba, apparently dating from the 600s on. Causeways run up to 5 or 6km from the central ceremonial zone to about a dozen other precincts. With perhaps 55,000 residents, Koba seems to have dominated Yucatan as far west as Yaxuna (see chapter 6).

CLASSIC PERIOD LIFE

Most Maya, like most other Mesoamericans then, before, and many still today, lived in single chambered houses of wood and plaster or mud brick (adobe) roofed with thatch. Commonly, the houses were protected from damp on plinths which, where ground conditions permit, are spotted easily by the archaeologist; but it is now known – with vexing implications for estimates of population – that not all were raised thus. Preserved under volcanic ash at Cerén are houses replete with pots in wall cupboards and kitchen implements – querns and a quern-stone have been found, and obsidian blades safely tucked away. Maya houses were probably for a couple of adults and their children; not roomy, but most activity would have taken place outside.

Beneath the floor or behind the house were often tombs. On rebuilding houses, offerings were made, as though to maintain the sanctity of the site. Perhaps, then, houses were inherited, as in Teotihuacan. To judge from most inscriptions on royal succession, inheritance would have run through the male line.

Houses stood, almost invariably, in groups of two to four, five or six, around a patio or yard. The Cuello site shows the pattern by 900 BC. For, as commonly today, presumably families comprised two or three generations together, each under its own roof. The kitchen was probably detached; and there were huts and pits for storage.

House groups were usually clustered, from five to a dozen or so, with an open space or plaza in the middle. Many of the plazas feature a mound at one side. Samples of these mounds have yielded burials more elaborate than those with the houses. If, then – as P.A. McAnany suggests – the mounds were shrines to common ancestors, clusters of houses may mark family lineages (she points out that that could be tested by examining the bones, as at Teotihuacan). Some clusters feature a larger house group, perhaps that of the senior living person. Finds at one of the larger eighth-century houses in Copan, including a typical Lower Central American tripod quern-stone, suggest a retinue of eastern immigrants. Around the clusters – just as, at different scales, around patio groups, villages and towns – are aprons of land which may pertain to the shrines or larger house groups. In some districts, bigger plazas with larger buildings are accompanied by a pyramid and surrounded by a great many house groups – the seats, perhaps, of grander families. At Copan, these groupings are paired, as though in 'dual' political and ceremonial organization. In general, however, where ground cover allows easier mapping, in both Yucatan and the highlands, it is striking that settlement is 'replicated' with regularity from house groups to plaza groups (see chapter 1); and, even without direct evidence, one can work out where the farms lay from settlement pattern, lie of the land and the distribution of water.

Archaeologists now appreciate that the social history was probably complicated if not also volatile. At Tik'al and Palenque, a middle social rank has been detected in burials of greater elaboration than most, but less than the royal tombs. In Tik'al's suburbs, some of the larger houses featured sculpted benches or 'thrones' reminiscent of the bench at Los Mangales and the Olmec 'altars'. At Caracol, housing, workshops and richly accompanied burials seem to reveal a middle order growing from the mid sixth century. The commemorative inscription of one leading suburban householder in Palenque acknowledges the king. At one large house in Copan, on the other hand, a burial and epigraphy seem to attest scribes or senior civil servants who were visited by the king in the later eighth century. Here and in another house, he acknowledged his hosts by blessing the place. The implications for the balance of power are intriguing (chapter 6).

A few seem to have lived more grandly in 'palaces'. One has been identified at Tik'al's Central Acropolis by its size and by an inscription. At Kohunlich, there was one for as many as 300 residents. At Kalak'mul, a smaller palace with evidence for skilled artisanry has been distinguished from a more elaborate one with richer household contents and a royal burial.

At Tik'al, bones reveal increasing distinctions of lifestyle corresponding to some of the differences in architecture and burial rites. W.A. Haviland & Hattula Moholy-Nagy have worked out that people buried with the grander houses tended to be taller and older. They may have enjoyed better diets: more animal bones are found at larger houses. Haviland & Moholy-Nagy found corresponding differences in leg musculature which they ascribe to sitting on chairs in the larger houses and squatting without them in the others. They also found that head shape varied with housing. Heads were shaped by pressing the forehead back in babyhood – a mark of distinction illustrated in the arts of the period. Haviland & Moholy-Nagy maintain that these differences began to emerge at the end of the first millennium BC. Later, head shaping 'trickled down' to ordinary people (although rare now, it is still done); but, while chairs were evidently adopted, in due course, by middling households, the humble remained without.

Most citizens lived in much the way of their rural cousins. As in villages today, houses would have had a kitchen garden, dogs, turkeys or ducks scratching about, and one or two trees for fruit and shade. The appurtenances are rarely preserved – beneath the ash at Cerén were found the little ridges and planting holes for crops – but they would help to explain the suburban spaciousness of Tik'al, Kalak'mul or Copan (*19*). Arthur Demarest argues that dispersion is fitted to the ecology of the rain forest; but how was the balance struck with the needs for aggregation?

The suburban gardens can have supplied no more than supplements. In places there were permanent fields and, in some hilly districts, terraces were built. Farmers in the Motagua and Ulua valleys of the south-east undertook both terracing and irrigation and also created plots in swamps by mounding dry ridges up. Near El Mirador, it looks as though gardens were made in dry ground by bringing in swamp muck. Caracol had terracing with scattered suburban farmsteads.

In the Peten, however, many of the cities were surrounded by swamps. There has been growing evidence that, as in the south-east, plots were raised at the swamps' shallow edges for seasonal or continuous cultivation. The method was known in western Mexico and along the Gulf coast (chapter 4; and see chapter 7). It was probably expensive in labour but highly productive – and, unlike milpa, not erosive. The edges of Pulltrouser Swamp, where the technique was practised, were heavily populated. A zone around Kohunlich is reported to spread over more than 200km^2; and drainage canals have been found in other parts of the central region.

Water too was a problem in Yucatan and the Peten. Some of the reservoirs and canals at Etz'na may have been for drinking water. The centre of Koba lay among lakes while Kalak'mul seems to have exploited natural ponds and, elsewhere in Yucatan, settlement was influenced by exposures of the watertable (cenotes) and enhanced by wells and tanks. Larger tanks were made at Tik'al and La Milpa partly by quarrying for building stone. At Tik'al, plastered plazas drained into reservoirs from which conduits led to surrounding house groups and fields. Indeed, the ancient word for plaza may have been 'lake'. Perhaps the aristocrats pretended to produce water through their observances at the pyramid-'mountains' among the plazas and reservoirs (compare plate 6).

'The lords . . . could not have done the work of building their houses or the houses of their gods, were it not . . . that their vassals had become numerous', explained the Popol Vuh. If only to ensure that the monuments were built, supplying the towns was surely a key aristocratic function. As at Monte Albán or Teotihuacan, rapid growth at Copan, Caracol or Río Azul, or the opposite at Tik'al, following victories or defeat, look like the effects of state action or decay.

The inscriptions at the 'scribe's' house in Copan indicate royal patronage; but did kings wield administrative power? The marsh reclamations could have been just local projects. Archaeologists have identified settlement hierarchies where, failing epigraphy, there is little to suggest dependence on a regional capital beyond. Around Tenam Rosario, Olivier de Montmollin has shown that, during the seventh and eighth centuries, local sites with ceremonial earthworks had comparatively big populations while relatively few lived at Tenam Rosario itself. Indeed, inspired, in part, by R.E. Blanton's analysis of early Monte Albán, he suspects that the layout of platforms and ball courts there was designed to acknowledge surrounding territories. As with the association of shrines and residences, the implication is that local social identities were strong. On the other hand research on farms in the district of La Milpa suggests that political integration depended partly on coordinating local specializations.

Yet the monuments of cities and district centres alike bespeak mass labour and, if only for symbolic effect, they tended to occupy nodal or prominent places, Tik'al and little Tenam Rosario on hills, for instance, La Milpa on a rise exaggerated by quarrying – the pits perhaps for ponds to complement the pyramids above – Koba among its lakes; and the discovery that, like the Sun Pyramid at Teotihuacan, a palace and shrines at Dos Pilas were sited above caves suggests that there was more to it all than mere 'effect'. Again, at Tik'al and Kalak'mul, common orientation of buildings well into the suburbs suggests symbolic unity (*19*). The inscriptions are full of information about relations between communities. Statements of allegiance to or overlordship by Kalak'mul in the 600s reveal a 'sphere of influence' embracing El Perú, Dos Pilas and Kankuwen. There are declarations of Kaminaljuyu's alliances with Piedras Negras, Seibal, Caracol and Quirigua; and references to war with Tik'al, Palenque and Tonina. For Naranjo, there are statements of both juniority to Kalak'mul and conflict with it. The other leading 'imperialists' of the day were evidently Tik'al, Palenque, Yaxchilan and Copan (*3*, *20* and *21*). At Naranjo, Caracol's stairway was evidently resented as an imposition; and it looks telling that, once Naranjo declined, its satellite, Xunantunich, was redeveloped.

POWER OR PROPAGANDA

How, then, did the Maya hold together? How did the aristocracy work? Was a middle order developing and, if so, was the simple cellular structure of society changing in some places? Or were there various forms of organization?

On the whole, it now looks as though states of the Classic period were confederations of local lineage groups, social 'segments' led, in the capitals, by headmen. Organizations of this kind flourished

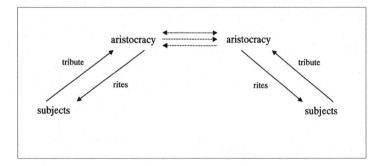

20 Classic Maya constitution: rites for tribute at home and reciprocation or extortion between states

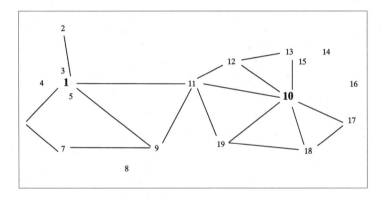

21 Map of associations among inscriptions: Tik'al and Naranjo in 731 (adapted from Marcus 1976). 1 Tik'al; 2 Waxaktun; 3 El Encanto; 4 Chikin Tik'al; 5 Uolantun; 6 Palmar; 7 Mejía; 8 El Gallo; 9 San Clemente; 10 Naranjo; 11 Nakum; 12 Dos Aguadas; 13 Holmul; 14 Yaloch; 15 Chunvis; 16 Bullet Tree Falls; 17 Xunantunich; 18 Tikinchakan; 19 Yaxha. Compare *17*

in Yucatan and the southern highlands at the time of the Spanish Conquest, albeit none as mighty as Tik'al's or Kalak'mul's. Such an organization, in which urban functions were loosely integrated, may help further to explain the open, rustic, look of the suburbs (*19*). It may also explain something of the period's glory and turbulence. The cities evidently compromised between local autonomy and the aristocrats' centripetal demands. Much of the iconography suggests

22 Altar Q at Copan, representing King Yax Pac's dynastic inheritance in 763

that, like Olmec chiefs' leaders had to justify their claims to power. The pervading idioms for authority were history, astrology and piety.

Seventh-century rulers of Piedras Negras insisted on com-memorating dynastic anniversaries. At Dzibanche, next to build-ings thought to have been palaces – but which could have been headmen's houses – the Owl Temple stood on a pyramid over a tomb. Palace and mausoleum certainly are juxtaposed at Palenque. At Tik'al, above both his father's tomb and the monument to Stormy Sky, Hasaw commissioned a pyramid and topped it with a temple. His own mausoleum was set adjacent (plate 16), and another one, perhaps that of his principal wife, opposite; his successors built more of these shrines. They seem to have been sited relative to selected earlier buildings by trigonometry. Yet, of course, however carefully represented, by themselves, genealogies begged questions: everyone had them. So it makes sense (as David Friedel & Linda Schele read the inscriptions) that, as in Palenque's Cross Group, seventh- and eighth-century kings should have claimed special efficacy for the spirits of their respective dynasties (22; compare 13).

More than just for genealogy, however, history was exploited to present rulers' deeds as inevitable or, cyclicity notwithstanding (chapter 1), unique. 'Twin pyramid groups' were built at Tik'al to mark the passage of time; and, at Piedras Negras, stelae were put up every five Maya years from 608 to 810. In 562, Caracol's retaliation on Tik'al was guided by astrology, a convention known to prehistorians as 'star war'. Hasaw's attack on Kalak'mul may have been timed to commemorate a deed of Stormy Sky's. At Palenque, a long inscription describes a coronation, in 721, with rites for the Sun that re-enacted, it was claimed, a ceremony 4000 years before. Koba's Stela 1 fixes a date in relation to a cycle of some 42 million[21] years! Royal patronage encouraged arithmetical sophistication.

Aristocrats seem to have claimed to maintain the world by divining its place in time and interceding with its governing spirits. At Yaxchilan, carvings recorded rites from the late seventh century to the mid eighth, including a wife of the king pulling thorns through her tongue, to draw blood for calling ancestors up (displayed in the British Museum). The sculptures on one building at Copan seem to represent the underworld and heavens, suggesting that that was where the city's later rulers undertook the same kind of duty. At Palenque, Pakal's tomb depicts the king as the best of all people and wearing symbols of the spirit of maize, descending the world's axis, a great ceiba tree, into Earth's skeletal jaws. The image evokes the afternoon Sun's descent to the underworld, while the pyramid rises above in nine tiers, presumably for the nine hours of night (a motif used for Hasaw's tomb too; plate 16); but the reference to maize suggests revival. The Cross Group develops the idea by arranging the shrines like the ancient triadic principle, the highest of them, at the north, in the direction of the ancestors, decorated as the 'sacred mountain': the noble dead ensuring life. It looks as though, in the central region, several ritual sites were laid out, in the Late Classic period, to emphasise a northern complex of buildings in relation to a complementary group at the south, with a ball court and causeways between them (23). An idea of the same sort may, long before, have dictated the position of Teotihuacan's Moon Pyramid, between the processional way and Cerro Gordo, or even the plan of La Venta (16, 12). Perhaps, then, for want of economic integration, Maya rulers depended on sacred rites for their authority.

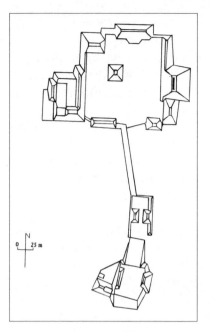

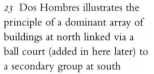

23 Dos Hombres illustrates the
principle of a dominant array of
buildings at north linked via a
ball court (added in here later) to
a secondary group at south

Converging with Michael Coe's comparison with the Khmer
(chapter 1), Prof. Demarest recommends the concept of a 'theatre
state'. It makes sense of the causeways built between the main
ceremonial buildings at Tik'al, probably in the mid-700s (*19*).Very
lofty pyramids were built too, perhaps to make the shrines more
visible – at almost 65m, Tik'al's Temple IV outdoes Teotihuacan's
Sun Pyramid. On the other hand, that made rites there remoter.
By the same token, palace and shrine were isolated together at
Caracol. Equally (questions of literacy aside), Classic inscriptions,
unlike the masks on Formative pyramids, were increasingly inac-
cessible. Some of Tik'al's stelae were hidden away among the
ceremonial buildings. Later inscriptions do mention officials and
craftsmen but the epigraphy was preoccupied more with nobles'
affairs than those of ordinary people. As explained by the theory of
the 'network' strategy (chapter 1), rulers reckoned power through
conventions of external relations: trade, perhaps, diplomacy, and
combat.

Trade in rare commodities was later an aristocratic pursuit and it may have been so in Classic times too. Sculptors and painters of the period were careful to depict the elite with ornaments of jade and showy plumes. Tik'al's conflict with Kalak'mul and Caracol may have been over trade in such luxuries. At Copan, imports from other Maya regions are rarely found outside the privileged city centre. From the other direction, whether or not obtained directly, a figurine of gold and copper was probably from 1000km away, but the considerable amounts of pottery from Lower Central America found in ordinary houses were evidently valued less.

Some scholars suspect that, from about 200 BC to AD 400, the highest title of honour rotated – perhaps in the sense of Prof. Lockhart (chapter 1) – between El Mirador, Kohunlich, Waxaktun and others, before Tik'al tried to keep it by assuming distant Teotihuacan's cachet. Contest thereafter may help to explain the records of dominance and fealty. The visit of a lord from Bonampak' to Yaxchilan was for homage, no doubt. Royal guests from Piedras Negras and even Tik'al were noted here too – would they have approved of the phrasing? A ball court at Kankuwen featured a stone showing a Ball Game between the king and visiting royal clients. On the other hand, Copan's Stela A boasts of parity with Tik'al, Palenque and possibly Kalak'mul in 731, associating each with one of the cardinal directions in order to claim 'world city' status. Evidence from the end of the Classic period in the Peten implies that authority was rotated according to a Short Count of 256 years; but was this modesty a symptom of strain?

Not content merely with giving their own blood, kings sought their rivals'. Caracol's standing was evidently much enhanced by killing the king of Tik'al. Perhaps, as, later, among the Aztecs, they were spurred by local leaders or growing retinues because victory brought plunder and tribute into circulation. Mobilizing followers to attack outsiders was probably one strategy that only the kings could manage. A good ploy it must have seemed for retaining the domestic political initiative; but it helped to undo them all.

Dark age or golden?

Teotihuacan fell in the seventh century. As though liberated, a series of flamboyant communities developed in vigorous exchange with each other between the old metropolis and the Maya. The loosely organized appearance of some of the towns must be related to the 'cellular' forms of society considered in previous chapters. They are reminiscent of the paradoxical concept of 'segmentary states' once proposed to explain certain societies in Africa. Barely a century later, the Maya began to abandon most of their cities and much of the countryside. The collapse of Classic Maya civilization remains one of the world's great archaeological mysteries. Can we work out which was more critical, the institutions of the state or the demands of urbanism? By 1000, a new influence, the Toltecs, was felt far and wide. The evidence includes both archaeology and legend; but this 'protohistoric' mix of sources proves difficult to interpret. The present chapter covers the end of the Classic period, the Epiclassic, and the greater part of the Postclassic, up to about 1300 (5 and 24).

TEOTIHUACAN

A haunting refrain in the Popol Vuh bemoans loss of linguistic unity among peoples formerly gathered at a capital remembered as 'Tulan' (Nahuatl 'Tollan'). Alfredo & Leonardo López think that it refers to failure of a union symbolized by the Feathered Serpent, an ideology perhaps first formulated at Teotihuacan.

The great city had not been in obvious trouble. Population had declined somewhat as people moved to the countryside but new

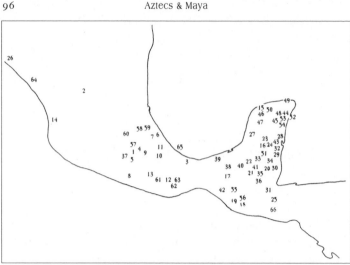

24 From the Late Classic to the Aztec era: 1 Teotihuacan; 2 La Quemada; 3
Matacapan; 4 Cholula; 5 Xochicalco; 6 El Tajín; 7 Yohualinchan; 8 La Organera-
Xochipala; 9 Cacaxtla; 10 Cantona; 11 Filo-Bobos; 12 Jalieza, Lambityeco, Monte
Albán; 13 Yucuñudahui; 14 Amapa; 15 Tz'ibilchaltun; 16 Tik'al; 17 Tonina; 18
El Baúl; 19 Santa Lucía Cotzumalhuapa; 20 Seibal; 21 Altar de Sacrificios; 22
Piedras Negras; 23 Kalak'mul; 24 Río Azul; 25 Copan; 26 Guasave; 27 Etz'na;
28 Santa Rita; 29 Lamanai; 30 Barton Ramie; 31 Quirigua; 32 Kolha, Nohmul;
33 El Perú; 34 Naranjo; 35 Dos Pilas; 36 Aguateca, Punta de Chimino; 37
Teotenango; 38 Palenque; 39 Comalcalco; 40 Pomona; 41 Bonampak', Yaxchilan;
42 Tenam Rosario; 43 Dos Hombres, La Milpa; 44 Koba; 45 Yaxuna; 46 Uxmal;
47 Kabah, Sayil; 48 Chichen Itza; 49 Isla Cerritos; 50 Mayapan; 51 Nojpeten;
52 Xelha, Cozumel; 53 Tancah; 54 Tulum; 55 Utatlan; 56 Iximche; 57 Tula; 58
Tuzapan; 59 Tantoc; 60 El Cerrito; 61 Tilantongo; 62 Zaachila; 63 Mitla; 64
Culiacán; 65 Isla de Sacrificios; 66 Cihuatán

buildings were being put up along the main avenue. Walls built
around the Citadel have sometimes been interpreted as defences.
Prof. Pasztory detects a new iconographic emphasis on individual
leaders. However, the walls may have been liturgical. Or, like the
contemporary Maya cities, they may indicate increasing social
exclusion. Some archaeologists see evidence in burials for widening
disparities of wealth. Arguably, late burials show some decline in the
complexity of rites; and some of the skeletons reveal malnutrition
and diminishing life expectancy. Was public consensus slipping?

1 At market in Antigua, highland Guatemala. The distinct patterns of weaving indicate that the older ladies and the young lady are from different villages

2 Coxcatlán Cave

3 Sowing maize in Central Mexico: seeds dropped into a hole made with the digging stick. The man at the back is in the region's traditional peasant whites, his young companions in modern style

4 Milpas, patches of temporary fields and fallow, in Guatemala

5 Colossal Head from La Venta (Villahermosa Archaeological Park)

6 'The King' at Chalcatzingo

7 Altar 4 from La Venta (Villahermosa Archaeological Park)

8 Monte Albán. The building in the foreground may be an observatory

9 Teotihuacan, the Pyramid of the Sun

10 Talud and tablero, typical batter and fascia in Teotihuacan

11 The Feathered Serpent on the Quetzalcoatl pyramid in Teotihuacan

12 A heavily bedecked spirit in Teotihuacan, dispensing bounty

13 Compound in Teotihuacan with a shrine in the courtyard

14 The western potter's art (Cambridge University Museum of Archaeology & Anthropology 1947.586; 1966.53A; 1966.55; 1964.124; 1966.536)

15 18 Rabbit, king of Copan,
hieroglyphs down the side

16 Tik'al's Temple I, Hasaw Chan K'awil's mausoleum, stelae at the foot

17 Palenque, the palace

18 Xochicalco, the Feathered Serpent platform. Note the fascia's projecting ('flying') cornice (compare plate 19)

19 The Pyramid of the Niches, El Tajín (with 'flying cornices')

20 Sacrifice of a Ball Game player at El Tajín: a skeletal spirit hovers as the victim is restrained and the knife poised

21 Uxmal – note the long-range structure

22 Chichen Itza: El Castillo, the Warriors Temple behind

23 Tula; in the foreground a ball court, and colonnade and 'atlantes' in the background (see plate 24)

24 The 'atlantes' at Tula

25 Tzintzuntzan: the royal mausoleum, Lake Pátzcuaro behind

26 Tlatelolco: the central pyramid revealing three phases of building, most of it having been sheared down in 1521; Colonial church in the background

27 Replenishing a chinampa with lakebed mud. The trees' roots hold the raised beds in place. A small zone of chinampas remains, partly now a popular boating park

28 Cholula, Colonial church atop the ancient pyramid

29 An early phase of the Aztec temple at Acatitlan, northern Mexico City, has been well reconstructed

30 Pilgrimage to Chalma (1930s). The staves and the boy's carrying strap or tump line were ancient travel kit

31 A Purépecha colleague of the author's responds to commercial demand with her Mesoamerican backstrap loom

32 Mesoamerica's future?

A couple of circumstances may have weakened the city. In as much as it depended on clients in other regions for imports, it was susceptible to disrupted links; and there is indirect evidence for that (see below). In the other direction, slight diminution of rainfall to the north may have started a press of 'economic refugees'. Around the Tropic, farms were abandoned during the 600s and 700s, some people apparently reverting to the Archaic life but others moving southward to districts better watered. The beetling ruins of La Quemada mark the eventual retraction of Mesoamerica's frontier.

Whatever the reason, the end came suddenly at Teotihuacan. Central parts of the city were sacked and burnt. The platforms in front of the Moon Pyramid and the steps to its summit were wrecked. The columns in the Feathered Butterfly palace, near by, were torn down. The main temples were looted and many of the ones along the central avenue and beyond heavily damaged. Life did not stop. Zones to either side of the main avenue either remained in use or were reoccupied; but decline of population increased sharply. By 950, it was down by at least 80 per cent, to about 30,000 in villages (one of which still flourishes). Yet, just as the city expanded by immigration, so now people dispersed across the Valley of Mexico. Clusters of villages and hamlets sprang up. Several towns grew nearly as large as Teotihuacan. A new cycle started.

CITY STATES

Directly or indirectly, Teotihuacan had been involved in the development of towns further afield. Among them, Matacapan foundered and Cholula may have faltered soon after the metropolis's influence waned. On the other hand, Xochicalco, El Tajín and others went on successfully to emulate the old capital; but they were much smaller and so were their respective 'spheres of influence'. New towns were founded too, such as Teotenango. There is also evidence to suggest states without cities.

Central to the process of 'secondary state formation' apparently stimulated by Teotihuacan seems to have been regional exchange. Indeed, the 'push' theory for the old capital's widespread influence (chapter 4) could allow that the city succumbed because it was deprived of imports by satellites usurping its networks: most regions in Mesoamerica have geographical alternatives among partners for trade; and shifts of initiative between 'core' and 'peripheries' are predicted by the economic theory of 'world systems'.

Supplies of obsidian at Xochicalco shifted from 80 per cent dependence on the sources near Teotihuacan to 85 per cent from the west, but the distribution suggests that this was not an effect of public policy. Xochicalco grew from substantial village to monumental town in the mid-600s. New ceremonial buildings included the batter & fascia, derived from Teotihuacan but with modification from the northern Gulf Coast ('flying cornice'; plate 18) and, or, the Maya, and elements of layout from the Valley of Oaxaca. Secondary centres elsewhere in the district exhibit the same eclectic synthesis. Appraising these and other influences in sculpture and pottery, some archaeologists consider that Xochicalco was a passive recipient but others interpret it as a meeting ground of privileged neutrality, while yet others credit the unknown rulers with appropriating foreign symbols for ends of their own.

Xochicalco overlooks a pass with long views to either side. Its 15,000 inhabitants did have gardens but they must have depended on farmers in the surrounding valleys. Roads led in from the hinterland. Other places in the district occupied defensive sites at this period too but Xochicalco is the only one surrounded by revetments and ditches. The most famous building is the Feathered Serpent platform, its batter decorated with the snake familiar from Teotihuacan and the fascia with the figures of soldiers (plate 18).

Perhaps, then, if trouble arose with the waning of Teotihuacan, Xochicalco was the district's citadel or hill fort. There may be an analogy with Monte Albán (chapter 4): Alfredo & Leonardo López read the reliefs on the Feathered Serpent platform as declarations of inclusive or federal authority. Yet the centre of the site was sacked and burnt in about 900.

The rough country to the south-west has long been known as the source of distinctive figurines in the elegant Mezcala style but, until recently, the material could not be understood because it had been torn out of the ground by looters – a practice perhaps dating back here to the Aztecs! Archaeological investigation has now assigned the figurines to the later first millennium BC; and digging the remains of buildings at La Organera-Xochipala has shown that, while the tradition did accept influence from Teotihuacan, it also drew from Oaxaca and the east coast and went on to flourish strongly between 700 and 1000.

Founded at about the same time as Xochicalco, and perhaps outlasting it by a century, was Cacaxtla. Decorating several of the walls of its formal buildings are brilliant, detailed paintings which combine stylistic and iconographic features from Central Mexico and the Maya. There are plaster reliefs in Maya style too. There are also traces of influence from the northern Gulf Coast; and some of the pictures are annotated with signs and numbers apparently derived from the Zapotecs.

Some of Cacaxtla's murals show bloody combat and warriors clad in jaguar pelts and feathers. These outfits and other motifs are familiar from both Teotihuacan and Aztec symbolism. Attributes of the Feathered Serpent feature prominently and war was a recurrent aspect of that spirit's cult. As at Xochicalco, Cacaxtla and contemporary settlements in the district occupy ridges. Cacaxtla itself is defended by ditches and at least one rampart.

Perhaps economic interests were at stake. For Cacaxtla lies by the 'Teotihuacan corridor' (chapter 4). One mural shows a Maya spirit with a carrying frame of the kind later called cacaxtli by Aztec porters. At the end of the ridge, overlooking the main route – from which travellers can see it clearly – Xochitecatl was incorporated as a suburban ceremonial precinct. Finds here included fine pottery from Teotihuacan, Oaxaca and the Gulf Coast. Legend associated the lords of Cacaxtla with the south-eastern Gulf Coast and with Cholula. It looks, then, as though they took over the 'corridor', developed Xochitecatl to display their claim, and invoked the Feathered Serpent to validate it among local contenders.

Some of the most remarkable discoveries of the 1990s were at Cantona, where survey on the ground and from the air revealed the remains of a town of about 60,000 to 90,000 people, the most populous known of this period. Spreading over 12km^2, it occupies a ridge crowned by groups of ceremonial platforms and 24 ball courts. People lived in small zones of houses grouped around patios or courtyards. The quality of housing varied from zone to zone. Lanes link different neighbourhoods.

Occupied from the early first millennium, Cantona grew in about 600 and boomed from 700 to 900. There was evidently a lot of obsidian working and, like Teotihuacan, Cantona seems to have commanded particular sources. Other goods came in from around the Gulf Coast, Oaxaca, and the north, including the Valley of Mexico, but Teotihuacan is not much in evidence. Indeed, the suspicion is that Cantona sought to wrest control of traffic between the metropolis and the Gulf Coast. The town was defended by ditches and it is thought that access both at the boundaries and along the lanes was controlled by blocks and sentries. Yet these precautions were to no avail in the end, when Cantona was overrun in the eleventh century, perhaps, like Teotihuacan, by immigrants.

The northern Gulf Coast followed a different course. As soon as Teotihuacan's influence faded, El Tajín grew, eventually to about 15,000 people. Its characteristic style of architectural ornamentation, sculpting and potting spread across the coastal plain and into the hills at Yohualinchan. Some archaeologists – and many local people – see it as the work of early Totonacs, the main Native group in the region today. Art historians have detected features of the style at Cacaxtla and Cholula; and it looks as though a colony may have been sent as far as Guatemala (see below).

El Tajín's centre has many pyramids and plazas, and unexposed earthworks all around show how much further the site extends. The Pyramid of the Niches has 364 little openings (plate 19). The Columns Building is a later structure decorated with scenes of rites, including a parade of captives for a noble or king called Thirteen Rabbit. However, the middle of the town was burnt down and abandoned by 1200.

El Tajín had at least fifteen ball courts. The South Court's walls are carved to show how matches ended with the execution of players for the benefit of the spirits who, for their part, were expected to ensure Earth's fertility (plate 20). Here and elsewhere in the northern coastal plain, many sculptures on the theme of the Ball Game have been found, court markers, 'yokes', and emblems known as palms. It is thought that the yokes were moulds for making leather pads to protect players from the heavy rubber ball.

At Filo-Bobos, investigations have revealed occupations from about 400 up to the Aztec period spread along a verdant valley now protected as a nature reserve. Two sites have been examined in detail: the Cuajilote complex, a series of ceremonial platforms and a ball court used up to the tenth century; and Vega de la Peña, a group of residential and ceremonial buildings occupied from about 1200. Research in the western part of the old Olmec 'heartland' has revealed a pattern of 'plaza groups' distributed at 6km intervals. It has been interpreted as a network of aristocratic estates. They may bear comparison with larger plaza groups of the Classic period among the Maya.

For the Valley of Oaxaca, the period from 700 to 1000 is not well understood. Aristocrats' houses and tombs were distinguished more than before even as central government decayed. By 800, the main plaza at Monte Albán was deserted and the largest town, Jalieza, did not have one. Yet the region maintained far connections. Pottery in Maya style was found at Lambityeco. A number of villages occupied defensible locations around the edges of the Valley, especially along westward routes into Mixtec country; and the Mixtecs themselves favoured defensive sites for towns such as Yucuñudahui and its satellites.

In the west, the Teuchitlán tradition lost its distinctive features of site planning between 700 and 900. However, villages and ceremonial centres continued and developed further west; and Colonial period temples of the Huichols, to the north, may have been derived from the Teuchitlán culture. By the ninth century, here, Mesoamerica's first metalworkers were making copper wire, needles, pins and hooks, small ornaments and little bells, and a few crescentic 'axe' heads. The latter were symbols well known in the Central Andes, but the bells were cast by the lost wax technique more characteristic of western Colombia and Panama. Finds of copper at Amapa, in tombs comparatively wealthy in pottery, hints at patronage of the new craft. It was the beginning of a fine tradition which, by the time of the Tarascan heyday, produced bronze tools as well.

After Teotihuacan, there was no unifying power. Both iconography and ruins do attest war but not enough is known about rural conditions to understand its wider effect. Yet this was no dark age. Kingdoms proliferated. As among the Maya, exchange thrived creatively between them; from the retreat of Teotihuacan to the waning of the Maya, it was more inclusive and intensive than before. Aristocrats and their clients throughout Mesoamerica shared much in common – laying the basis for the 'Toltecs'.

THE MAYA COLLAPSE

One by one, nearly all of the Maya towns in the central region and the highlands were abandoned. Starting in the 760s, the clearest evidence is their final inscriptions. Palenque's was made in 799 and Kalak'mul and most of the other western towns fell still by 811. In the south-east, recording ceased by 860. At Tik'al, it continued until 879, at three towns to its north ten years more and, at Tonina, another 20. Surveys show that the south-western highlands were largely deserted; and population in the Valley of Guatemala seems to have fallen by more than 80 per cent, as much as during the early Spanish period. Many attempts have been made to explain the 'collapse', invoking cultural factors, natural factors, or combinations of both at either regional or local level.

One approach is to blame immigrants fleeing the upheavals in the west. Distinctively elegant but harsh sculptures from El Baúl and other sites around Santa Lucía Cotzumalhuapa, in the southern lowlands, depict aspects of the Ball Game and its associations with the spirits of the cosmos and with death. They are reminiscent of the preoccupation at El Tajín. Among the inscriptions, numerals are expressed in Mexican fashion, not Maya. The date is in doubt: some archaeologists associate the sites with the Teotihuacano pottery from the district to the west (chapter 5); but most consider that they are of the ninth century. Some, in turn, suggest that they mark the arrival of Pipil, a language close to Nahuatl, still spoken here and in pockets to the east, associated by archaeologists with slightly later buildings and artefacts at and near Cihuatán; but others suspect that the Cotzumalhuapans were Putun, Maya from the district around Comalcalco. In any case, the evidence affirms a continuing connection between the south-western Maya and the Gulf Coast (compare chapter 3).

The Putun are attested along the Yucatan coast in about the ninth century, apparently spreading as traders. Stelae of this period at Seibal exhibit features found in the paintings at Cacaxtla and elsewhere in the west; and a western technique of fine paste pottery was introduced here and at Altar de Sacrificios. Accordingly, some blame the fall of the western towns on the Putun. Perhaps they were the vandals who pulled monuments down at Piedras Negras and smashed the pieces. Yet one stela at Seibal seems to claim association with leading Maya capitals (including Tik'al and, apparently, Kalak'mul) in the same way as had Copan's Stela A (chapter 5). Failing better evidence for immigrants, it is simpler to suggest that Seibal and Altar were partners in the exchange flourishing to the west.

At Río Azul, the whole town was wrecked. It is thought to have been invaded from the north. Northern influence appeared at Nohmul too but here it is associated with restoration of the town, deserted since the fifth century. Copan's, on the other hand, was a story of neglect, not destruction. There were immigrants but not among the aristocrats (chapter 5), and decline is not attributed to invasion here.

How else, then, could the collapse be explained? Local reasons were various, no doubt, but there were probably general processes behind the pattern of extinction. The seventh and eighth centuries saw peaks of population, at Tik'al and Copan, for instance, La Milpa and Nohmul, all coinciding with massive programmes of monument building. The south-western highlands had been densely settled. Tik'al was already declining earlier in the 800s. Pollen from the Peten lake district attests weeds and trees colonizing the fields. Research at La Milpa suggests that farms struggled with soils impoverished by excessive use and, around Copan, abandoned housing implies that soil was exhausted or eroding under cultivation or stripping for wood. Human bones from Tik'al, Altar de Sacrificios, Kolha and Copan indicate malnutrition. At Tik'al and Copan, mortality was unusually high among infants and adolescents. Some evidence from Tik'al suggests cannibalism.

In places, the concentration of population looks defensive. Dart heads found in the ruins of Yaxchilan's acropolis suggest a final assault. Inscriptions at Dos Pilas indicate that war started, in the mid-600s, under a scion of Tik'al's royalty who launched a campaign of aggrandizement, including alliance with Kalak'mul and possibly El Perú,

marriage with Naranjo, and a raid on Tik'al itself. In 735, a successor captured the king of Seibal in 'star war'. In 761, however, rebels
caught and sacrificed the king of Dos Pilas and the town was razed
amid desperate street fighting. Villagers cleared some of the damage
up and may have been joined by others from the countryside; but
the court seems to have retreated to the naturally defended site of
Aguateca. Both civilian defences and fortresses were built in the
surrounding district. At Punta de Chimino, a pair of deep moats
were cut to make an island of the site. Some archaeologists surmise
that these disturbances provided the opportunity for the Putun to
interfere at Seibal. Yet war did not affect everyone alike: there is no
evidence of malnutrition in this district; and, while, at Kolha, two
mass burials of aristocrats mark the end in about 800, life in surrounding villages was unaffected at first.

In 711, the king of Palenque was captured and killed at Tonina. The
picture of him there carved in the distinctive style of Palenque itself
may have been demanded from his own retainers. The same irony
shows in a stela, at Piedras Negras, showing captives taken in 'star
war' from Pomona in 794. Apparently, then, war did affect courtly
dependants as well as their patrons, if not commoners too. Murals at
Bonampak' show more of what went on, depicting a coronation in
790 and the events that followed over the next two years: a procession – including a rare reminder of music – battle, the display, torture
and beheading of captives, and a rite in which the royalty sacrificed
blood of their own. (The paintings have deteriorated but are reconstructed at the National Museum of Anthropology in Mexico City.)
The palace at Palenque exhibited low relief sculptures showing captives and tribute borne in from poor Pomona. At enemy Kalak'mul,
prisoners were depicted in a rock carving.

A small range of rooms built on the acropolis at Copan in 746
implies that such antics were losing credibility. The building is decorated with herringbone work that is thought to represent matting for
dignitaries to sit upon. There is a similar find from an earlier period
at Waxaktun. In the early 1500s, at Utatlan, in the southern highlands,
headmen met in long buildings set on platforms; and, in Yucatan,
such council halls were called 'mat houses' (for their seating; see
below). Other motifs from the same façade at Copan may represent

particular families. Rubbish discovered near by shows that feasts may have been given here. The suggestion is that, no longer able to unite them against common foes, the king commissioned the building for consulting and perhaps honouring the heads of local families. The visits to their houses by his predecessor, the flamboyant '18 Rabbit', may have been the first sign of royal failure (chapter 5; plate 15). In 738, 18 Rabbit was caught and sacrificed at Quirigua, perhaps (suggests one hieroglyph) with Kalak'mul's backing. A stairway and temple were added to the acropolis with a long inscription defiantly reciting the Copan's royal history; but it was poorly built. The last dated inscription was cut – but not finished – in 822.

Yet the surrounding villages grew. What collapsed at Copan – as in Kolha too, perhaps – was federal organization or perhaps the tributes that supported it (20). Rural decline did set in during the eleventh century but the villages seem to have persisted to about 1300. At Palenque, the concentration of population relaxed in the later eighth century: people dispersed into the hinterland, as though asserting peasant independence. Similarly, perhaps, recent survey near Dos Hombres has revealed a zone of small households established rapidly in about 800, apparently managing water collectively without a site hierarchy.

Some people lingered among the crumbling pyramids at Tik'al. Nohmul lasted into the eleventh century, Barton Ramie into the twelfth; Lamanai contracted but survived into the Spanish period; and life went on at Santa Rita Corozal and surrounding villages as well. These occupations in Belize seem to be associated with influences or even immigrants from the north and perhaps also refugees from the west. A few small towns did develop likewise in the Peten; and some land near Aguateca was put to use for the first time in the tenth century.

Whether or not villagers did manage to disperse, urban life failed in most of the central region. There are no clues, other than some evidence for immigrants in El Salvador, as to what befell the highlanders. Nor was the problem only Maya: a well populated district a hundred miles east of Copan was deserted by 1000. From Chiapas to Honduras, the country was abandoned between the ninth century and 1200.

Probably, the Maya collapsed, in one district and another, for various related reasons of political organization and agricultural management (25). True, their history was long a process of continuity through political instability, like the Olmecs: both the south and the central region underwent upheavals in the third century, and cities rose and fell thereafter too; but the ninth century may have brought a concatenation of factors that undermined the capacity of towns – and, apparently, villages too, in the end – to recover.

Even if the citizenry did not feel ignored by Late Classic royal ritual, one grave challenge to aristocratic claims of competence may have been the climate. There is widespread evidence for a cult of caves – long associated with weather (plate 6) – which seems to have intensified during the eighth century. Increasing waterside settlement at Dos Hombres may indicate drought.

For Yucatan, information on water life and chemistry has been collated with data from other parts of Mexico, Central America and around the world to confirm that drier conditions set in from about 850. Exceptions in the Peten may merely confirm that drought was the basic problem: the new towns there lay beside the lakes. Northern Belize may have been saved by its rivers and by coastal trade. Recent research on the chemistry of human bones suggests increasing reliance there on seafood.

YUCATAN

By contrast with the rest, the northern Maya underwent marked development, some of it almost certainly on account of immigration from the central zone. Circuit walls suggest that the change was fraught. In about 800, a causeway was built from Koba all the way – over 100km – to Yaxuna. It may have been a response to the growth of towns in western Yucatan. The biggest of them was Tz'ibilchaltun, estimated at 25,000 inhabitants, but grandest was Uxmal (plate 21).

The impression of Uxmal's importance is borne out by a causeway to Kabah, where the terminal archway can still be admired. The central buildings in these towns are in the Puuk

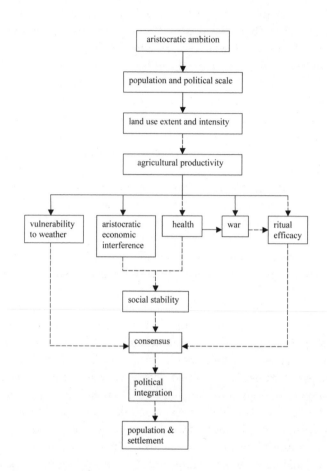

25 Causes of the Classic Maya collapse according to David Webster (broken lines show conditions for deterioration; see References)

style (chapter 5). Like the earlier Chenes style, it is intensely ornamental. The repertoire included motifs familiar from the west; and M.E. Miller has pointed to sculptural conventions reminiscent of eighth-century work in the region of Yaxchilan. The most distinctive Puuk buildings are 'range structures' (plate

21). The array of doors could be merely a function of architectural technique but, like the 'mat house' at Copan, they may distinguish the chambers of federated headmen. The distribution of buildings and 'altars' at Sayil implies that political and ritual authority was dispersed, not concentrated exclusively at the 'Great Palace'; but, at Uxmal, the biggest ranges feature a central door that is larger and, or, distinctly marked. If that distinction was for acknowledging the king, was it, then, that his role was yet weaker than it had been in the south or that the principle of federation was stronger?

During the eighth and ninth centuries, one of the principal towns was Chichen Itza. Its main buildings lie near a vast natural well, the Sacred Cenote, into which, during later centuries if not already at the end of the Classic period, were thrown jade, copper, gold, and people – offerings, presumably, for ensuring the supply of water. In the town, imported pottery has been found, including wares from the Gulf Coast and Plumbate ware from southern Guatemala. The imports could be explained by a local tradition associating the town with the Itza, Putun refugees from the Peten. A wall painting and a gold disc found in the Cenote show crews paddling canoes. One suggestion is that, in order to exploit local salt, they established a beachhead with a harbour at Isla Cerritos, where pottery from both the Gulf of Mexico and the Caribbean has been found. Were the Itza trying to develop coastal trade in compensation for a former overland route in the south (chapter 5)?

The southern part of Chichen Itza – including a distinctive round building commonly interpreted as an observatory – was in the style of the period, but the buildings of the northern part, occupying a massive platform near the Sacred Cenote, are different. The Castillo is a pyramid of nine stages (compare chapter 5) with 91 steps up each of its four sides (plate 22 ; the play of shadows along them at the spring equinox now attracts crowds of New Agers). Its previous phase was ornamented with images of jaguars and snakes and the final phase has a statue at the top, of the type known as chacmool and associated with human sacrifice. To the east lies the Warriors' Temple, ornamented with Feathered Serpents, and beside it spreads an immense colonnade. To the other side of the

Castillo is, among other features, a gigantic ball court. It is decorated, like El Tajín's South Court, with a scene of human sacrifice,
snakes and vines spurting from the victim's neck. Adjacent is a
wall decorated as a rack for skulls. Close by is the Cones Platform,
which resembles Xochicalco's Feathered Serpent platform.

Partly on the basis of Yucatec legend, the 'New' north zone was
long attributed to the Toltecs of Tula, far to the west; but detailed
reassessment of the archaeology shows that it is contemporary
with the south zone and earlier than most of Tula. Chichen Itza
is all Maya. The New zone is merely a much larger version of the
adjacent part of the 'Old', surely intended as a complement or
contrast – a response, perhaps, to the same problems overwhelm-
ing the cities to the south, perhaps a fundamentalist gesture, like
Pharaoh Akhenaten's Amarna. Nor was the New style necessarily
so original: it was probably part of the aristocratic military idiom
common in so much of Mexico.

Yet, in the end, the strenuous symbolism was to no more avail
here than down south. Signs of pillage confirm the account of
later chronicles that Chichen Itza was attacked. One reading
assigns this event to 1221 but it is unlikely that the town lasted
that long. Pilgrimage continued but then seems to have diverted,
for a time, to the cave of Balank'anche, 4km away. According to
legend, Chichen Itza's court eventually made its way to Nojpeten
(Tayasal), in the Peten lake district. At Koba, declining maize pollen
confirms that activity diminished there but people did manage to
stay there among their lakes until about 1400 and, latterly, rebuilt
the shrine atop the biggest of the Classic pyramids.

A new capital was founded in the thirteenth century at
Mayapan. Its population is estimated at 15,000. The central zone
includes a pyramid like the Castillo at Chichen Itza and a hall
where councils may have met; but the buildings are small and
flimsy. There are about 15 range structures, perhaps for local lineage groups. Although they would have run farms outside, the
town was enclosed by a wall, its meandering course apparently
intended to surround certain of the site's natural wells. Adding
to the sense of defensiveness, housing was denser than in other
Maya towns. Lavish military burials accord with later chronicles'

account of tyrants exacting tribute from neighbours until deposed
in the mid 1400s.

By the time of the Spanish invasions, Yucatan comprised about 16
aristocratic domains. Like Classic kings, some lords acknowledged
others as paramount but the peninsula was not unified. Nobles
enjoyed trading all the way around from the Lago de Términos to
Honduras. The coastal sites of Santa Rita Corozal, Xelha, Tancah,
the walled village of Tulum (now a favourite tourist draw), and
the shrine at Cozumel each show connections with the rest of
Mesoamerica in the fourteenth to sixteenth centuries.

TULA

The Toltecs were literally larger than life, according to the Aztecs.
Toltec (toltecatl) means master artificer in Nahuatl: they were credited with superb skills. As the epitome of civilization, the Toltecs
were associated with Tollan, image of the 'golden age' city, and Aztec
antiquaries sought relics of them in the ruins at Tula, and probably
Teotihuacan too.

In 1941, scholars established the orthodoxy that Tula was the
Toltec capital. Archaeologists came to regard New Chichen Itza as
a Toltec colony, and sought the Toltecs throughout Mesoamerica.
Historians joined in by scouring sixteenth-century documents. The
combined results suggested that Tula anticipated Aztec imperialism.

Tula had been occupied in Teotihuacan's heyday but, from the fifth
century, there is a distinct pattern of finds and, as in further districts
of the Valley of Mexico, population grew following the metropolis's
decline. Some archaeologists consider that the pottery of that period
was derived not only from Teotihuacan but also the north-west –
further evidence, perhaps, of 'economic refugees'. Many villagers
took to the hills around Tula, as though in defence.

In about 950, the middle of Tula was moved to where the main
ruins lie today. The population, by 1100, was up to 60,000. The
town was laid out on a grid plan. Most people lived in small compounds. They had shrines of their own but there were little street-
side temples too – compare Loma Torremote, 2000 years before.
The ceremonial centre does resemble New Chichen Itza but it is

smaller (plate 23) – and visitors should note that archaeological reconstruction of details was modelled on the Maya monument!

Another 50,000 lived in surrounding villages. Housing at Tepetitlan was of the same kind as in Tula, although other buildings there, not yet investigated, look different. The villagers used various kinds of maize but lack of the diagnostic crockery suggests that they did not make the 'tortillas' so essential to Aztec and later meals. They seem to have eaten less rabbit than the town dwellers but the find of a fragment of cacao shows that they benefitted from Tula's distant connections.

Like New Chichen Itza, the architectural ornament and statuary at Tula is sanguinary and militaristic (plate 24). Directly and indirectly, it refers to human sacrifice and the spirits for which the immolations were made, notably aspects of the Feathered Serpent. Legend confirmed that there was a cult of this spirit here. The principal pyramid was surrounded by columns. Some scholars discern the prototype of this colonnade at Alta Vista in the north but the same feature is found at the Warriors Temple in Chichen Itza. Among the columns were set chacmools.

Tula's influence has been found in neighbouring districts, notably in the lay-out and design of the smaller centre at El Cerrito; but some archaeologists regard the military theme as the clue to a set of architectural and sculpted motifs and pottery wares and designs distributed all over Mesoamerica from about 950 to the later 1100s. Pot somewhat akin to Tula's is found at fortified sites such as Tuzapan. One archaeologist claimed to have detected the retreat of defending Totonacs there. However, beyond north central Mexico, the case for imperialism is weak. First, there are marked regional variations in the architecture and sculpture. Secondly, key types of pottery – Fine Orange, glazed Plumbate wares and Papagayo Polychrome – come not from Central Mexico but from the southern Gulf Coast, Soconusco and southern Guatemala, and the Nicoya Peninsula, respectively (compare Chichen Itza). Nor do they form a quantitatively coherent distribution. Nor, Chichen Itza aside, is evidence for conquest as clear anywhere else as in the northern Gulf Coast area. Nor even are all of the 'Toltec' attributes found at Tula itself.

It begs fewer questions to suppose that earlier trade had created channels for the diffusion of favoured goods and symbols – the 'Teotihuacan corridor', for instance, the Pacific seaway, or the route around Yucatan. Warlords may have exploited parts of the network on behalf of Tula or for themselves, but that cannot account for the whole pattern of Toltec evidence. The problem is like that of the Olmecs' influence or Teotihuacan's; and it can be solved as follows.

PRESTIGE AND AUTHORITY

Along the northern Gulf Coast, distinct from the Tajín tradition and the Totonacs, was the Huastec culture, discernible with archaeological evidence from the tenth century and still flourishing in the Aztec period. It is noted for sculpture which includes ritual themes of life and death and the passage of time, some of it faintly reminiscent of the Olmecs. There were several big ceremonial centres such as the ancient site of Tantoc. Relatively little research has been carried out but it is known that circular platforms are comparatively common which, elsewhere, were associated with the Feathered Serpent as spirit of the rainy season easterlies. Spanish explorers in 1518 reported a round tower on the Isla de Sacrificios, where pottery from many parts of Mesoamerica has been found, much of it probably from burials. The island may long have been a shrine to the Feathered Serpent.

Cholula, if it did falter when Teotihuacan declined, had more than recovered by the time of the Aztecs. Its cult of the Feathered Serpent was a source of authority for the region's governors, who were ceremonially fitted out with emblematic nose studs. Cholula was a major pilgrimage destination too. The Epiclassic Patio of the Altars shows affinities of ornament from both the northern Gulf Coast and western Oaxaca. The main pyramid was enhanced during the last centuries before the Spanish invasion. Lots of Mixteca-Puebla ware, the finest pottery in Mexico, was used; indeed, it was probably first developed in or near Cholula. In about 1200, in the Valley of Mexico, between Cholula and Tula, there was a zone little settled, like a buffer between two powers.

Similar evidence has been found from about 900 onward in the western valleys of Oaxaca. The Mixtecs here made less use of defensive sites than before but towns like Jaltepec maintained hill forts adjacent. Chronicles confirm that it was a time of wars. Some of the places that they mention have been found and it has been shown, between Jaltepec and Tilantongo, that settlement diminished as the fighting increased.

The best known story in the Mixtec chronicles is the life of Eight Deer, ruler of Tilantongo, who undertook a series of alliances, diplomatic marriages and conquests before he, in turn, was captured and sacrificed, probably in 1063, whereupon his domain disintegrated (26). Eight Deer's and other Mixtec dynasties claimed descent from the Feathered Serpent. They said that their ancestors travelled to a place of authority, and Eight Deer did likewise to receive a nose stud of turquoise.

At the same time, Mixtec pressure on the Valley of Oaxaca's broad acres was increasing. The Valley was divided into about 20 principalities, with Zaachila preeminent in political standing and Mitla in sanctity. Long wary of the mountain men, the Zapotecs built defences for Mitla, Jalieza and other centres but, by the mid fifteenth century, Mixtecs had settled more or less throughout the Valley.

The Mixtecs had taken up metalworking and excelled at it. Their most gorgeous treasure yet found accompanied a collective burial. It included gold, silver, turquoise, crystal, amber, jet, coral and pearl, along with fine pottery and engraved bone. Mixteca-Puebla motifs feature clearly; but, as though historic local associations were needed too, they used an older Zapotec tomb on Monte Albán (Tomb 7; the finds are displayed in Oaxaca City's fine Cultural Centre).

In the south-east, Toltec symbolism was as prominent in the revival and development of the mountain Maya as it had been in Yucatan. The Popol Vuh tells of princes who travelled to a destination that sounds like Tula or Teotihuacan. There they acquired patron deities. The K'ich'es' was the snake-footed god of the dark mirror that had been claimed by kings in the central region during the Classic period (and perhaps much earlier at Izapa). This spirit instructs the K'ich'e to conquer and make tributaries of their victims. The lords then travel again, apparently now to Chichen Itza, where they gain both wisdom and royal titles including Mat Keeper and Reception

House (tribute warehouse) Mat Keeper. In due course, both titles were taken by a figure with shamanic powers, named Feathered Serpent. His successors, explains the Popol Vuh, extended K'ich'e dominion and developed Utatlan (K'umarkah), from the early 1400s, as a veritable Tollan.

Later parts of the story correspond to a couple of previous capitals which have been found by archaeologists. Archaeology also confirms the Kaqchikels' story of breaking free from the K'ich'e and setting up their own capital; and, elsewhere in that region, other capitals have been investigated. Like Yucatan, most of these sites have 'big house' ranges suggesting segmentary political structure, and their pyramids exhibit Central Mexican design. Secondary sites clustered around Utatlan express the play of centralization and fragmentation in the same way as the layouts of Tenam Rosario or Monte Albán (chapters 5 and 4). Survey around them, in turn, has found smaller villages, at least as many as there are today. Consistent with the Popol Vuh is the tendency to occupy defensible sites. Some of the capitals look practically impregnable. Recovery since the Classic period had been rapid and disturbing.

As in Teotihuacan's day, demands for 'prestige goods' stretched well beyond Mesoamerica. Beginning in about the eleventh century, turquoise was imported in increasing amounts from New Mexico, Arizona and Utah, where the Pueblo Indians used it too. From the same period, tropical feathers, little copper bells and mirror backs of Mexican iron have been found among the ruined villages in Chaco Canyon, New Mexico, and elsewhere in the region. Archaeologists have speculated as to whether trade helped to stimulate development there or whether these exotic goods were used to bolster chieftains' claims on power. The whole range of southern imports has been found en route at Paquimé (Casas Grandes) along with Feathered Serpent symbolism; but finds in Arizona imply that there may have been a western route too, from Guasave. Some archaeologists discern Mexican influence in mounds and iconography all the way from the Arkansas River to Georgia. By 1300, Arizona and New Mexico succumbed to drought but the turquoise still reached Central Mexico over the next couple of centuries.

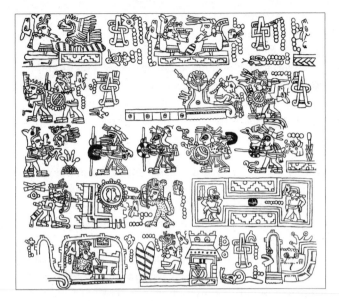

26 Mixtec chronicle: the Bodley Codex. The military idiom is typical.
Eight Deer (deerhead with eight dots) is mentioned six times. The 'A'
signs mark years. Note Mixteca-Puebla 'greca' or 'step-fret' ornament;
and Ball Game at lower right

From Tula and Culiacán to Iximche' and the Caribbean,
common decorative motifs and iconography were wrought in
precious metals and gems, painted on pottery and in the books of
the Mixtecs and the Puebla basin, and painted or sculpted on walls.
They were still current in the Aztec period. Art historians often
refer to the pattern as the Mixteca-Puebla style. Never excluding
local traditions, it stood out as an 'international style'. Typical of
the 'network' strategy (chapter 1), it expressed Mesoamerica's plural
integration. Cholula and Chichen Itza, above all, contradict the
notion of a single 'Toltec' Tollan at Tula.

THE IMAGE OF THE TOLTECS

Tula was burnt in about 1170, probably in a series of incidents.
Some occupation continued but the town lost its grandeur. The

Aztecs had a legend that helps to account for the debacle. The great king, Topiltzin, they explained, was corrupted by the sorcery of the spirit, Tezcatlipoca. To the king's aid came the Feathered Serpent, who joined him in exile, away to the east, promising one day to return (hence, perhaps, the cult on the Isla de Sacrificios). The tale of Topiltzin may be a memory of faction and coup d'état. Perhaps the disturbances were caused by new waves of refugees from northern drought.

What is to be made of the Toltecs? The usual account describes a development akin to both Teotihuacan's and the Aztecs' to follow, implying cycles and constraints in Mexico's ancient history, corresponding, perhaps, to balances of power between neighbouring regions with complementary resources. If, however, Tula was but one power among others, then there was a single cycle of political integration from the fall of Teotihuacan to the rise of the Aztecs. Toltec mythology and the ideology of the Feathered Serpent were not Tula's own, then, but Teotihuacan's rehearsed in perhaps three or four Tollans, most notably Cholula, perhaps Xochicalco, El Tajín, Chichen Itza, and perhaps, indeed, Tula.

Like Teotihuacan's and the Olmecs', Toltec style was an idiom of prestige. It was like the Maya conventions of trade, diplomacy and combat (chapter 5). In particular, it looks as though the cult of the Feathered Serpent was exploited in attempts to unite communities for whom local or family identity always came first. Aristocrats visiting any part of Mesoamerica will have seen the style and recognized it; but that does not imply political unity.

What about their subjects, though? Perhaps the nobles overlooked them but have archaeologists too? The results of the surveys in the Valleys of Mexico and Oaxaca and in the Mixtec valleys are full of implications, while the investigations at Filo-Bobos and discovery of extensive settlement on the Gulf plains now suggests that the eastern lowlands were a distinct hearth of civilization. Meanwhile, we know only that 'For the upper classes all periods . . . have been golden, for the masses none' (D.N. Jha).

The Aztecs and their enemies

On the eve of the Spanish Conquest, western Mesoamerica was dominated by two powers, the Mexica (Aztecs) in Central Mexico and the Tarascans (or Purépecha) in the west (27). Because they held sway over the biggest population in Mesoamerica, the Mexica drew most of the Conquistadors' attention; and they have preoccupied scholars and popular imagination since. In many or most respects, of course, Mexica life and thought were like their neighbours', including the Maya, so that it is worth describing it in some detail; but, in studying the Mexica as typical Mesoamericans, it is necessary, in places, to mark differences. Equally, while much of Aztec life was like their ancestors', it was distinct in certain ways.

The name 'Aztec' refers variously to the Mexica and their neighbours in particular, to most or all of the Indians of the Valley of Mexico, and often to related peoples in neighbouring parts of Central Mexico too. It will be used in the broadest sense here; but, at the time, the term had special connotations and, for the Mexica and their cousins, more specifically, 'Nahua' would have sounded right for most purposes.

OBSCURE RISE, UNCERTAIN APOGEE

By 1500, the leading figures in Central Mexico were the Mexica of the city of Tenochtitlan. They claimed to have inherited the tradi-

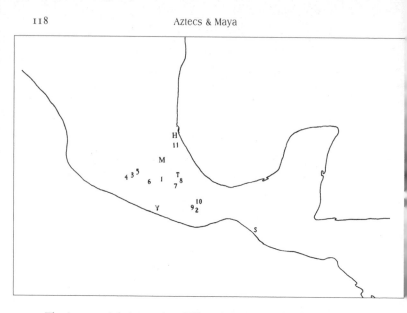

27 The Aztecs and their enemies: 1 Valley of Mexico; 2 Zaachila; 3 Tzintzuntzan; 4 Pátzcuaro; 5 Ihuatzio; 6 Calixtlahuaca; 7 Atlixco; 8 Cholula, Huexotzinco; 9 Huaxyacac; 10 Ixtepeji; 11 Castillo de Teayo; H Huastecs; M Meztitlan S Soconusco; T Tlaxcala; Y Yopes

tion of the Toltecs, whom they eulogised as paragons. Tenochtitlan, then, was the ideal city, the new Tollan, and the Mexica themselves were the contemporary epitome of how people should live (28).

Yet, in the approved account, the Toltec inheritance was indirect. It was usually said that Tenochtitlan was only founded in 1325 or even 1345. Historians described a fitful process of political alliance and administrative reform, thereafter, by which the Mexica became versed in Central Mexico's 'great tradition'. Their earlier whereabouts and way of life, they explained, were quite the antithesis of the Toltecs, their ancestors Chichimecs, barbarians!

Urged on by their patron spirit, went the story, the Mexica left 'Aztlan', an arid land far to the north ('Aztec' means 'people of Aztlan'). Drawings of the trek depict priests carrying bundles of sacred items of a type also shown in Mixtec books and mentioned as ancestral accoutrements in the Popol Vuh. Known as 'medicine bundles' in the North American Plains, they are typical of the Archaic heritage (and some are still kept today). Arriving in the Valley of Mexico, almost two centuries later and after lots of adventures, they found many prior immigrants and had to plead for land. They survived by dint of inherited hardiness. Even the twin isles of Tenochtitlan and Tlatelolco, when first they were allowed to settle there, were just rocks.

Were the tale to be believed, our humble barbarians then took little more than a century to become the Valley's leading power. Yet details reveal long familiarity with the Valley's or the Toltec tradition. This is not to deny that some key event took place in about 1320. There are archaeological traces in Central Mexico of immigrants from the north and west during the period described by the Mexica (chapter 6). In part, at least, the contradiction can be resolved by allowing that the account acknowledges an immigrant contribution to the Mexica stock. By 1300, every group in the Valley of Mexico must have comprised a mixture. Similar stories were told in the Valley of Puebla, and the Tarascans too claimed Chichimec founders. However, in 2008, remains perhaps as early as the 1200s were discovered beneath Tlatelolco's central shrine.

Why – whatever the chronology – did the Mexica revel in their Chichimec heritage as well as glorying in the Toltecs? The paradox has to be understood in the light of the rest of their turbulent history and of their view of the world.

During the 1300s, Tenochtitlan was just one among dozens of small towns in the Valley. Emerging pre-eminent, in the 1360s, were the Tepanecs of Azcapotzalco and the Acolhua of Texcoco. Whether or not they prosecuted their own as well, as increasingly senior clients of the Tepanecs, the Mexica contributed to military campaigns both in the Valley and, by 1400, in Morelos, to the south. There were similar cycles of rivalry and dominance among neighbouring peoples throughout Mesoamerica. In the mid 1400s, the Zapotecs of Zaachila were equivalent to the Tepanecs and, like them, they attempted to conquer further afield, in the Tehuantepec district. Subsequently, they were confined there and displaced from the Valley of Oaxaca by the mountain Mixtecs. However, in the Valley of Mexico and among the Tarascans in the west, the cycle was transformed.

In 1418, the Tepanecs overcame the Acolhua and made them pay tribute, including some to the Mexica. Eight years later, however, a coup in the Tepanec palace produced a regime unfavourable both

28 Aztec history, according to Codex Mendoza, showing foundation of
Tenochtitlan (the legendary leader dignified with fringed cloak and a mat) and
subsequent conquests (below; note temples ablaze). The surrounding cartouches
record the years' passage. A sign for the New Fire ceremony marks the third
from right in the bottom row

to a faction of Tepanec nobles in the small town of Tlacopan and the Mexica; and when the new ruler resumed hostility against the Acolhua, the aggrieved made common cause in a 'Triple Alliance'. With help from Huexotzinco, they overran Azcapotzalco in 1428.

Whether by virtue of their role in defeating the Tepanecs or of the political dexterity of the Tlatoani (king), Itzcoatl, and Tlacaelel, his premier, the Mexica emerged as leaders of the Alliance and the Valley of Mexico's principal power. They then carried out a series of social and constitutional reforms; and, as customary among the Aztecs, after important changes, the official history was retrospectively revised. Over the next two decades, the Mexica duly set about consolidating and extending the Tepanec domains as their own, in the Valley, in Morelos, and yet further afield. Moreover, the Allies were soon courted to intercede in others' struggles, and they took such opportunities to assert their authority over the arrangements that they brokered.

The Mexica were checked in the early 1450s. For then the rains were meagre and crops failed; and it happened again, the next year, early frost or drought ruining the crops, and the year after that. The Tlatoani exhausted his stores for the needy. People scavenged in desperation. Children were sold to households that could feed them; adults pawned themselves as slaves. Some emigrated to the abundant northeast coast, apparently helping to extend the distribution of Nahuatl (2). The pyramid at Castillo de Teayo may be their monument.

1455 brought a full harvest at last. It was, doubtless, with tremendous displays of civic affirmation that the Great Temple in the middle of Tenochtitlan was reinaugurated; and there followed reforms in government policy, at home and abroad. The Mexica reorganized the Valley of Mexico by posting collectors among the other towns, levies on which were mostly staple comestibles. Then, in 1473, Tenochtitlan annexed Tlatelolco by force. Political relations between the two isles had long been ambivalent and the Tenochca were probably jealous of Tlatelolco's valuable tributaries and its merchants' success in trade for precious commodities. The coup probably disrupted a traditional ritual relationship between the isles; but the combined effect of these moves helped to confirm Tenochtitlan's political and economic supremacy among its allies.

More important for the rest of Mesoamerica was that, in 1458, the army was launched on a campaign of conquests further afield. Like the new temple, it may have been intended to impress the public with the efficacy of their governors. Claims that 200,000 soldiers were committed confirm that appearances mattered! The muster would have been exciting for every campaign, and the victors' return with booty and lines of prisoners was orchestrated, no doubt, to look and sound stirring. Enemy resistance and counterattacks prompted further action.

There may have been an economic strategy at work too. The first long-range attack was against the Huastecs of the bountiful east coast. During the drought, their neighbours, the Totonacs, had brought grain for sale to the Valley of Mexico. Cynics suspect that the Huastecs were a soft target; but the intention may have been to ensure reliable access to the lowlanders' resources. Likewise, later attacks on the Tarascans are interpreted by some scholars as a drive for access to minerals.

Subsequent campaigns extended the Allies' control but the costs rose. For, firstly, the longer range expeditions, south-eastward, were difficult to sustain. Secondly, expansion to the west was blocked by the Tarascans. Comparatively little is known of Tarascan history but, by the last quarter of the 1400s, Tzintzuntzan had been promoted as capital over Pátzcuaro and Ihuatzio and the Tarascans were forging an empire of their own, partly, perhaps, in response to the Aztec threat. In about 1480, they decimated the Allied army, and the frontier remained in stalemate thereafter – the hapless Matlazincas there repeatedly recruited or trampled by one or the other foe. Third, the Aztecs were successfully resisted by Meztitlan, in the north, and the Yopes, in the south. Fourth, there was chronic war with the Tlaxcaltecs, who had become the leading power in the Valley of Puebla. The engagements against them and their allies came to be called 'Flower Wars', to connote formality and ritual; but the suspicion is that the Triple Alliance was simply unable to prevail. The Allies resorted to siege but, in 1515, both sides suffered heavy casualties at Atlixco.

Further changes of policy were made during the reign of Motecuhzoma (Montezuma) II, from 1502. Privileges that had proliferated among both nobles and soldiers were cut back while, on the other hand, the etiquette surrounding the Tlatoani was elaborated and the role of premier diminished. Motecuhzoma was evidently a tyrant. At the same time, he asserted himself increasingly over his two allies.

ORDER IN A TEEMING LANDSCAPE

The major feature of the last two centuries before the Spanish Conquest (as too now) was burgeoning population. The Valley of Mexico was transformed by the spread of settlement and farms (*29*). The growth of Tenochtitlan, in particular, was like Teotihuacan's, except that the Mexica metropolis did not empty the countryside. Similar growth took place in the Morelos basin and, almost certainly, elsewhere in the central highlands, although without such intense urbanism. In Morelos and around Tzintzuntzan, there are signs that soils were deteriorating under excessive cultivation. One technique adopted widely for pre-serving the soil was to terrace the slopes; and the Tarascans managed some of their lakeside fields as permanent plots.

Immigration did contribute to growth in the Valley of Mexico but could only have accounted for a fraction of it. Yet, if, before, Toltec organization was undermined by settlers, the Valley's new-comers may have stimulated changes in political organization which allowed development. Whether or not its roots were older, the key institution to emerge was the civic community, 'city state' or, in the Nahuatl, altepetl, meaning 'water-mountain' - an old cosmologi-cal concept (chapters 1 and 5). Each had its own laws and seat of government, central shrine and, in most cases, main market. Cycles of alliance and negotiations for patronage and clientage must have been continual. Mexica legend shows as much. The aristocrats of Culhuacan were said to be descended from the Toltecs and affili-ation with them lent special kudos. The main form of political relationship, regional or local, public or personal, was tribute.

As their city rapidly grew, Mexica politics must have become complicated; but Tenochtitlan could not have existed without countryside. Like the other peoples of Mesoamerica, that is, indeed, where most Aztecs lived; Mexica customs were rooted in rural

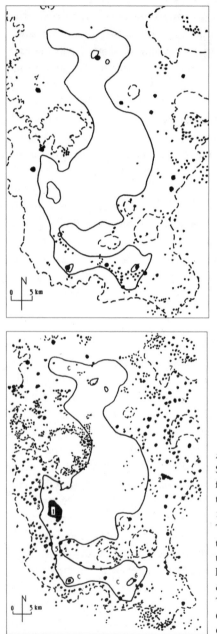

29 The rise of the Aztecs (after Sanders et al. 1979 [reference for chapters 3-4]): settlement in the Basin of Mexico in about 1250 (top) and 1500 (bottom). The continuous line marks the lake edge, the broken line the foot of mountains. In the lower map: 1 Tenochtitlan & Tlatelolco; 2 Texcoco; 3 Tlacopan; 4 Azcapotzalco; 5 Culhuacan; 6 Xico; 7 Cerro Gordo; C chinampa zone

tradition. At the eve of the Spanish Conquest, the basic social unit
in most or all of Central Mexico was a group of families which
owned common land and regulated its own affairs. Like the altepetl,
and for the same reason, it maintained a shrine of its own. The
Aztec version of this institution was the calpolli. In the modular or
replicative turn of Mesoamerican thought, the word was used for
communities at various scales, depending, apparently, on context.

   Another of these ideals seems to have been endogamy, the principle that families should seek brides among other families in the
same calpolli. The bride would commonly leave her family to live
with the groom's (*30*). This norm makes sense for farming: marriage
within the calpolli helped to retain the estate intact; and, since it
was the men who worked the fields, selection of brides should

30 Wedding at an Aztec home (Codex Mendoza). Note the distinct seated
postures of men and women, the seating for the men and honoured couple, and
the 'speech scrolls'

have helped to maintain families and their respective allotments alike. That may have become critical as the countryside filled up. Indeed, some families evidently fared better than others, ranked higher, and probably sought marriage partners from equivalent families. In contrast, the Cuicatecs, in semiarid country with less predictable weather, redistributed land every year.

Archaeological excavation of rural houses has shown that they were small buildings grouped around the yards where most home life will have taken place (30). Early Spanish surveys of suburban Mexico City confirm that most house groups had outer yards, used as kitchen gardens. Nahuatl terminology for kin helps to show why houses were arranged around inner courts (31): that the same words were used for siblings as for cousins suggests that related families tended to live together. In several parts of the world, including the contemporary Nahua countryside and eastern Guatemala, 'joint families' have proved well suited to working shares of collective land.

Survey at Cerro Gordo revealed the layout of a village displaying the typical features of a calpolli (32). House sites were found, most with terraces adjacent, probably for kitchen gardens. Larger platforms were presumably for leading families. Shrines were identified tentatively too. The village lay around a couple of streams, giving it a double form that makes sense of the principle that people married within their calpolli. Between the streams lay a pond and a couple of larger, presumably communal, buildings, including, perhaps, the calpolli's school. Michael & Cynthia Smith surveyed the remains of a much smaller village in Morelos lying along a single stream but also in two parts with larger buildings between them. These layouts are reminiscent of the early village at Coapexco (chapter 2) and perhaps analogous to the paired settlements at Copan (chapter 5). Were they merely effects of topography or did people expect to settle in paired groups? Did calpollis use symbols like the paired motifs found in Oaxaca's early cemeteries (chapter 3)?

In practice, there must have been a lot of variation in the formal and informal lives of calpollis, not least in response to economic conditions. Elizabeth Brumfiel has shown that, near Texcoco, textile spinning declined during the later Aztec period while work on maguey fibre and maize increased. Similar evidence for cottage

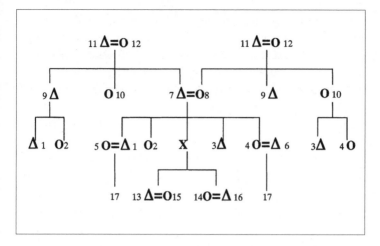

31 Aztec kinship classification. X husband or wife addressing the others; man; O woman; = married to. Each number represents a single term, e.g. 1 for 'teachcauh', elder brother or cousin

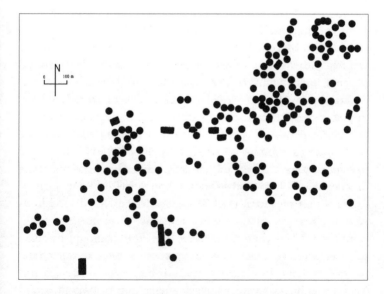

32 Aztec village at Cerro Gordo: two clusters of houses and other features with four larger buildings between (after Evans 1985)

industry in maguey has been found at Otumba near Teotihuacan.
Dr Brumfiel ascribes these changes to the development of markets
at the cost of local self-sufficiency; and she collates this pattern
with increasing proportions of domestic figurines of women and
temples to argue that worship too was affected by the state's ideology. There was a similar change in supply at Xico (*29*), which, she
argues, was caused by despatch of tribute to absentee lords; but here
there was little change among figurines. In Morelos, the Smiths
have shown that, at the same time, more obsidian and pottery was
imported from the Valley of Mexico while exchange within the
district declined. For the district around Texcoco, R.E. Blanton
suggests that the government redistributed local markets for
political ends.

Beyond their family's requirements, men up to the age of 52
owed part of their work time (a corvée) to the calpolli – usually,
when they were less busy in the fields, during the dry season –
for projects such as repairs to terraces or irrigation channels. The
calpolli, in turn, was required to contribute work to projects of
the local lord's or the municipality; it was the unit for recruit-
ment to the army too; and it was exploited for levying tribute
to the lords. Indeed, the usual word for the member of a calpolli
was macehual, literally subject or vassal. This is a decidedly 'Toltec'
concept, implying that there had long been lords or chiefs; but had
clientage always been the lot of calpollis or was it a later adaption to
the more crowded landscape or an attempt to discriminate immigrants? Some calpollis seem to have been administrative creations
set up by lords or landowners. In parts of the Valley of Puebla, rights
to land may have depended not on membership of calpollis but
on clientage to lords with estates, although both the members of
calpollis (not necessarily called macehuales here) and local lords
were liable to pay tribute to their respective governors.

In theory, Tenochtitlan's calpollis formed four groups or quarters (*28*). This mode of organization is well attested in other parts
of Mesoamerica. In certain districts of both central Mexico and
Yucatan, authority rotated annually among four communities; and
a similar arrangement may have obtained long before in the central
region of the Maya.

At the eve of the Spanish Conquest, there were about 50 city states in the Valley of Mexico, perhaps a similar number in the Puebla basin, and 70 in Morelos. These statelets varied greatly. In the Valley of Mexico, other than Tenochtitlan, the biggest town was Texcoco, with some 25,000 people; and there were about a dozen other centres with populations of 10,000-15,000, and many others with only about 5000. Nearly all were surrounded by satellite communities. The pattern was similar in the Valley of Oaxaca except that there were no large towns.

Tarascan government was quite different. By means both political and economic, the king controlled a hierarchy of officials from metropolitan nobles to village headmen. They organized the collection of maize, cotton and other crops grown on state fields by people contributing their labour as a public tax; the officers raised troops, and they administered justice in the king's name. The capital's principal monument is a platform supporting a row of lavish tombs (plate 25).

Archaeological survey in the Valley of Mexico has revealed a couple of zones not conforming to the model for calpollis and their local centres. Here, instead, there were only scattered farmsteads. It is known that some nobles had private estates: the unusual pattern may be the effect of intensive farming by dependent tenants. In fact, one of these areas, the 'chinampas', is comparatively well understood and has even been interpreted as a state estate; but that is best explained in connection with the peculiar conditions of Tenochtitlan.

TENOCHTITLAN

'Some of our soldiers asked if what they saw was a dream', said Bernal Díaz of the Spaniards' first arrival in the Valley of Mexico. A century before, just one among many towns in Central Mexico, Motecuhzoma II's capital was, by then, much the biggest city in Mesoamerica, indeed in all of the Americas. With Tlatelolco, it had some 300,000 residents. More is known about Tenochtitlan than anywhere else at the time; but, as in most big cities (though not necessarily earlier Mesoamerican towns), traditions were surely

changing. No doubt, that was one reason for older Nahuas' emphasis on propriety in describing their former way of life to the
Spanish.

Looming 35m over the centre was the Great Temple. Enlarged
three more times since 1454, it was surrounded by other shrines
and ancillary buildings. Traces of them and devotional sculptures
are often unearthed (4); and, in 2007, archaeologists found what
they suspect is the tomb of Ahuitzotl, Motecuhzoma II's predecessor. Other pyramids rose from the ceremonial precincts amid each
of the four quarters stretching around the centre, and another great
pyramid stood over Tlatelolco (plate 26).

The main streets were broad and straight but they must have
been crowded. Leading in from the lake, there were canals on
which heavier loads were borne in canoes and punts; and the
city was also linked to the surrounding shores by causeways with
sluices. Side streets led into different quarters, some full of workshops, others mainly residential, some wealthy, some poor. Small
towns, like Azcapotzalco, were probably laid out in grids too and
will have been similarly differentiated.

Most Mexica lived in households like their rural cousins'.
Density of population was higher than in older cities but the suburbs were notably green, thanks to the yards. Many houses were
decorated with family emblems. The nobles lived in mansions;
and the Tlatoani and premier kept palaces near the Great Temple.
Motecuhzoma II's palace included warehouses where tribute was
gathered.

The Tlatoani was at once governor of the city and of all
Mexica domains beyond. For, in theory, Tenochtitlan was the
model for the rest of the world; and, in practice, those domains
simply served the requirements of Tenochtitlan itself. In theory,
again, government was by consent, as in rural calpollis and in
chiefdoms of old, the Tlatoani consulting a council of repre-
sentatives of the city's four quarters. 'Tlatoani' means speaker:
by implication, he did not command, except in his role as army
chief. In practice, however, the inner council is likely to have
been appointed, not elected; and it invariably included members
of the royal family.

Kitchen gardens notwithstanding, the economy was different, perforce, from the countryside. Many men made their living as porters. Certain quarters were given over to manufacturing. Different, again, some artisans seem to have been exempt from the local labour draft – though not from levies on their products. Was economic specialization transforming the 'cellular' mode of organization (chapter 1)? There are hints that the process was already a matter of policy by the early 1400s.

Providing water and food was a special problem. Aqueducts were built from beyond the opposite shore. Nezahaulcoyotl, Tlatoani of Texcoco, commissioned one both to provide drinking water for the city and to maintain the canals; but, in 1499, a new scheme caused severe flooding. The market at Tlatelolco was reckoned to swarm with 20,000 people daily and at least twice that every fifth day. Here, geography helped: it was easy to punt supplies in bulk across the lake and along canals into the centre. More came in as tribute from beyond the Valley of Mexico.

One stretch of country probably especially dedicated to supplying the great city was the southern chinampas. Chinampas are garden plots built up from a shallow lake bed (plate 27). They were similar to the earlier Maya raised fields and those in the Teuchitlán area. Chinampas were made in several parts of the Valley of Mexico's lake, including the suburbs of Tenochtitlan itself; but the biggest stretch was in the southern district covering some 120km². With intensive husbandry, this zone may have yielded as much as half of all of Tenochtitlan's food. It is thought that most of the chinampas were made during the mid 1400s – perhaps in response to the crisis of the 1450s. Nezahualcoyotl is credited with contributing a barrage to protect them from the saltier part of the lake. The southern chinampas are one of the anomalous areas of dispersed settlement: the pattern may have been planned, without regard to calpolli custom, for more efficient access to the fields by labourers.

IMPERIALISM

The Mexica extended their demands for tribute across half of Mesoamerica. Much of the action was symbolic but the underlying reasons were economic and political. The longer range conquests, from 1458, could be cases in point of the ecological interpretation of Mesoamerican history. The methods of Tarascan imperialism were different, although its basic functions probably the same.

The methods and the limits of imperialism depended, in part, on earlier cultural history. By the 1500s, Nahuatl was spoken in many parts of Mesoamerica and used widely as a trade language and lingua franca. To a point, no doubt, that is a measure of the Allies' strategic success. Zapotec nobles near the garrison at Huaxyacac (Oaxaca) were proficient speakers. Yet, earlier western influence among the highland Maya, for instance, implies that the Aztecs expanded their power where there was already a tradition of contact with Central Mexico (although there was intriguing variation in 'Mexican' influence between, for instance, the K'ich'e and Kaqchikels [chapter 6]). Equally, the distribution of Mixteca-Puebla art, hardly a popular genre but still flourishing, traced a network among aristocrats. By contrast, Tarascan (Purépecha) was restricted to the west; nor did Tarascans indulge in Mixteca-Puebla style.

Among the Aztecs and other nations in Central Mexico, imperialism was, in large part, an affair between nobles, not whole populations. It was probably the same with warfare among the ancient Maya. So how much effect had this game on commoners? The opening gambit was usually a gift or a request from one of the Allied Tlatoanis to the lord of a city state. Acceptance implied a debt, payment of which was construed as political submission. Often, therefore, the gift was haughtily rejected. Diplomacy ensued while soldiers were mustered. War would follow and, on winning, the Alliance set terms of tribute; and the army marched home with booty and captives.

No stipulations were made as to how the tribute should be collected and delivered and few imperial officials stayed. Only rarely was a garrison left or were colonies sent from the Valley of Mexico. There was normally some manipulation of local allegiance by means of aristocratic honours and even marriage but, otherwise, the Alliance interfered little in domestic affairs. For the tribute acknowledged a relationship between one or other of the Allied Tlatoanis and the local lord. Some dues may have been distributed so as to disrupt local political allegiances. Indeed, dues were not always clear: once their own lords acknowledged two powers, the Zapotecs of Ixtepeji claimed to lose track of their obligations!

The Tarascans, by contrast, may have been forging a territorial empire. After some 90 years of plunder and discontinuous conquest beyond the Pátzcuaro basin heartland, policy crystallized in about 1440. Their language was promoted and colonies were routinely settled in an attempt to influence non-Tarascans. Four administrative seats were sited near regions where further expansion was sought. Although recently annexed territories were ruled through local nobles, the intention, here too, was evidently to incorporate them, eventually, in the centralized regime. The coastal Mixtecs as well were forging a small empire but, although they appointed a few local administrators and maintained some garrisons, their mode of indirect rule was akin to the Aztecs'.

Considering that the Aztecs usually respected local autonomy, were they imperialists at all? The tables of the Mexica Tribute Register show that some demands were so heavy that local effects may have been extensive (33). It is not clear to the European reader whether every community was liable for the whole amount in its table or whether the burden was shared across a province; nor is the frequency of liability always clear. However, on first landing at the Gulf coast, the Spanish soon discovered that the few resident Aztec officials were detested. Archaeology in Morelos seems to reveal some of the impact of tribute. The Smiths found here that spinning increased after the Aztec conquest. The fabric was almost certainly cotton; but the workers themselves probably dressed in rough maguey. Cotton was one of the principal commodities demanded as tribute; Morelos was one of the Aztecs' main sources of this material; so, after the conquest, ordinary people probably had to work more on making cotton cloth. Nor did indirect rule necessarily preserve their lords' privileges: the Smiths have shown that the comparatively affluent houses – presumably elders' – were relatively smaller after the Aztec conquest and that their standard of living declined more than in ordinary houses.

Indirect ('hegemonic') rule was inefficient in some ways. Whether on account of resentment at the burden of tribute or of

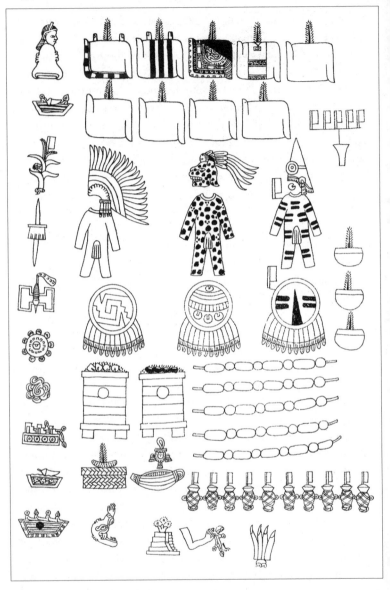

33 Tribute owed to the Aztecs, including cotton cloaks, at top, and military costumes and shields (Codex Mendoza). Down the left side and along the bottom are listed towns from which they were due. The Codex copies the Mexica Tribute Register

local lords trying to keep the enhanced revenues for themselves, there were many bids, by the Huastecs and Totonacs, for instance, to throw the Aztec yoke off. So the Allies had to undertake fresh expeditions against rebels. On reconquest, yet heavier tribute was demanded. On the other hand, the Allies seem eventually to have contained expenditure by limiting war beyond the tributary zone. Along the Tarascan front and the eastern flank of the Tlaxcaltecs, and around the Yopes and the coastal Mixtecs, a series of provinces was made to commit not only goods in tribute but also military manoeuvres, as though to distract the more dangerous enemies. The Tlaxcaltecs, in turn, if not the others, tried to turn these pawns against the Triple Alliance.

Tribute was like blood. Had it ceased, the Tlatoanis would have faced a 'legitimation crisis' (see References), threatening their authority at home. Like the Classic Maya rulers, they depended on precious resources from abroad. For, in part, the regular flow satisfied a philosophical requirement; and, in part, it helped to meet a pressing economic requirement. The latter is easier to explain first.

As the web of tributaries spread, three factors transpired among the demands. Allowance was made for the effort of haulage: bulk goods such as food and timber were ordered from closer to the Allies' capitals, and lighter more precious goods such as gold or plumes from further away. This distinction may correspond to the difference, developed in the 1460s, between close administration of tribute in the Valley of Mexico and less direct regulation further afield. Whatever the motive behind the first great conquest of the Huastecs, most of their tribute, 60 years later, was lighter than corn. On the other hand, ecology came into the calculation too: most of Huastec country, for instance, is hot, and they had to send cotton which grows well there but not in the Valley of Mexico. Equally, Soconusco was seized from the K'ich'es, in 1510, probably, in part, to secure supplies of cacao, which grows there – beans used as currency, or brewed to make what Nahuas called chocolatl. The principle was qualified in some cases by demands for goods which could not be procured within a tributary's own territory. For instance, the jadeite or greenstone required from Soconusco probably had to be obtained by trading to the east. Thirdly, the value of the tribute was not merely utilitarian but symbolic too. Varieties of cotton cloak and various costumes or decorations were required from most tributaries (33).

Which of these factors was the most important and how did the command economy mesh with the market's supply of food, cotton or wood? The same questions arise from the archaeologists' analyses of local changes in rural supply. One answer tends to emphasise the ecology, another the symbolism. For the Mexica, the most telling clues are the textiles and ornaments. They were needed by the rulers for their scheme of awards for service and for rewards and payments to the corps of state officials, which had grown with imperialism. Certain jewels for the ear or lip were reserved as decorations for soldiers, other insignia for government officers. Demand for such items must have seemed doubly ironic to the conquered.

The state rewards also included cloaks. For cotton cloaks (as well as cacao beans) were used as currency. Different qualities of fabric and manufacture bore different values. A macehual's cost of living was equivalent to about 20 standard cotton cloaks a year. The price of a slave ranged from 40 of the big capes down to eight. It is likely that these cloaks entered the market as privileged and wealthy households bought supplies or services.

The relation between state and private sector was complicated by the pochteca, merchants who specialized in long distance trade and who supervised markets in the Valley of Mexico. Unrelated to the tribute economy, they were purveyors of luxuries to the wealthiest; and the Tlatoanis seem to have invested in some of their expeditions, perhaps from their stores of tribute.

The pochteca may have been used to collect intelligence from beyond the Alliance's provinces. At least one expedition was provided with guards; and at least one attack on pochteca was treated as an affair of state, although they also proved capable of defending themselves against sustained onslaught. The pochteca maintained a guild. Their main feast fell on a day regarded by others as most inauspicious. Reputedly wealthy, they entertained the elite; but, under the sumptuary rules, they concealed their riches and, unlike the army, on returning, they stole their cargoes in by night. The ambivalence probably indicated strain between formal public institutions and new unofficial activities thrown up by social and economic change.

Supplied, thus, from the warehouses of both state and pochteca and from the ordinary markets, there was a rapid turnover of food and textiles ostentatiously given out, in age-old fashion, by grandees and leading citizens at public celebrations, holidays, and private banquets. With the same connotations of patronage as the Tlatoanis' to foreign lords, these presents helped to set up and maintain networks of obligation.

'Who's who?' and 'Who's whose?' were always at issue. Tenochtitlan was a vortex of ambitions which whirled across all Mesoamerica. Two of the most notorious features of Mexica public life – war and sacrifice – can be explained in part by the governors' attempts to control this process.

WAR AND SACRIFICE

War served four purposes for the Aztecs and most of their neighbours. The evidence of the Classic Maya and the emphasis on war during the late period in Teotihuacan and in Central Mexico thereafter shows that these goals were not new but one of them, in particular, was probably especially intense among the Mexica.

The most obvious purpose was strategic. The Allies' campaigns against the Mixtecs and Zapotecs, for example, were intended partly to outflank the enemy in the Puebla Valley and partly to secure access to the southern Maya.

Secondly, at its best, battle was art. Regiments swept upon each other yelling. From a little distance, it must have looked balletic once the crack legions were committed (though, to be sure, the generals preferred not to risk them!). Tall standards and drums signalled manoeuvres. The soldiers were kitted out in splendid colours (33), their bodies commonly painted too. The elite wore superb compositions of feathers, designed for flowing movement and the play of light.

The costumes of two of the leading Mexica regiments indicated what this art was for. The 'eagle men' wore the feathers of that rapacious master of the sky, the 'jaguar knights' the pelt of the master of the night. Other armies deployed similar symbols. These soldiers impersonated elements of the cosmos. Like the Ball Game, the battle fought properly was a rite. The priesthood, members of which fought alongside the soldiers, promoted war. The Mexica patron deity was god of war.

The third purpose was ritual too. Aside from opportunities for more mundane trophies, the soldier's aim was not to kill but to capture. Schoolboys were taught how to do it. For the objective was to bring the prisoner back for public sacrifice at the principal shrines – a cache of 70 skulls found at Tlatelolco confirms that the heads were then exhibited. Captivity and sacrifice were formalized – followed, in some rites, by eating parts of the body. It was an ancient practice and there were versions of it elsewhere in the Americas.

The government is said to have cultivated the 'Flower Wars' as a hunt for sacrificial victims. Aristocratic sculpture reveals a shift of emphasis from war as such to sacrifice as the reason for war, corresponding, perhaps, to difficulties during the last two Tlatoanis' reigns, and to the change noted by Dr Brumfiel in figurines.

The fourth purpose was probably emphasised far more by the Mexica than others. It followed from sacrifice but, as well as its religious function, it helped, like tribute but directly, to satisfy social ambitions. There was an award scheme. Rules on hairstyle, clothing and jewellery were used to distinguish army veterans and to mark a series of feats up to the achievement of four captures. That accomplishment qualified them, in turn, to attend councils of war and serve in senior offices either military or civilian. Top officers were also granted the use of estates. In part, the scheme turned on the distinction between nobles and commoners; for the macehual, battle was almost the only way to cross it. There may also have been pressure from leading citizens for the benefits of booty. Soldiers, for their part, counted on it – 'many', remarked Diego Durán in his history (1581), 'ate only when they went to war'. Finally, for the Mexica – as too, perhaps, for Teotihucan long before (and for Rome, or other societies since) – war probably combined ritual with another social function: although Mexica battle tactics did preserve distinctions between calpollis, militarism encouraged common goals and a standard of values or kudos reflected, for example, in public prominence given to leading soldiers.

So war was in demand at Tenochtitlan. After Motecuhzoma I (d. 1468), who had launched the army on its long range mission, Tlatoanis marked their accessions with conquest. Tizoc proved ineffective, jeopardising the flow of tribute, and died after only five years (1486), possibly at the hands of his staff. His successor, Ahuitzotl, invited enemies as well as the citizenry to attend his coronation, making sure to distribute ample largesse. He then led the army out to revive the Aztec claims, and reinaugurated the Great Temple by sacrificing the captives. However, Motecuhzoma II retrenched opportunities for office, reinforced distinctions between nobles and commoners, and tried to limit advancement by abolishing the honours for four captures.

Thus, war satisfied several requirements; but the danger was that excessive emphasis on one set among its complementary principles would unbalance the whole system of values. It may have been the same among the ancient Maya.

THE GODS

Owing to Spanish concern, a lot is known about Mexica religion and, by extension, Mexica cosmology or worldview. One of the challenges, however, scarcely acknowledged by either the Spanish or more recent scholars, is to recognize how beliefs and practices varied between different groups and strata of Aztec society and, thus, to appreciate the Indians' political values as well as their spirituality.

Aztec prayers were offered like promises in a bargain with the spirits; but it was always for people to beseech. For the spirits had created the world through sacrifice. Mortals had to acknowledge this: worship and sacrifice, in return, were duties. There was a balance to maintain. Sacrifice was for the gods as tribute for the state.

The proposition was that people have a spiritual anatomy of connections with the surrounding world. It was served by divination and prayers which involved aspects of astrology and psychology. There were rituals for achieving contact with various forms of spirit; and aristocrats were held to be especially effective at these rites. The spirits, for their part, could make themselves known. There are similarities with Hinduism; and, as with that religion, the principles worked, in cellular fashion, for householders at home as for high priests at major temples. The Spaniards' investigations, research in archaeology and epigraphy, and anthropologists' discoveries among contemporary and recent villages confirm that much the same held throughout Mesoamerica.

The easiest way to review Aztec religion and cosmology is to start by considering Mexica myths of creation. The Legend of the Suns (chapter 1) was probably as ancient as Mesoamerica; but there was a specifically Mexica version of it which is also revealing. It explains that the Mexica patron deity, Huitzilopochtli, Hummingbird On The Left, was conceived by the Earth. Earth's many other children, especially the Moon, suspected that the baby was illegitimate and plotted to kill him; but Huitzilopochtli emerged ready armed with a fire serpent and slew them all, dashing the Moon, in particular, off the mountain of Earth. The well armed iridescent Hummingbird is the Sun which scatters the sky's lesser lights, Earth's other children, at dawn with his beams and then courses forward to the left, the south, of the zenith (in the northern tropics, of course, the Sun appears south of the zenith for most of the year). His moral for the Mexica was that to fight is to live. That was how he urged them on from Aztlan. The Mexica Sun was a war god.

The story of Huitzilopochtli was represented on the south side of the Great Temple of Tenochtitlan. At the foot of the steps there, beneath a shrine to the god, lay a low relief sculpture of the Moon shattered by Huitzilopochtli's attack. The pyramid itself, then, represented the Earth upon which the god was born.

The neighbouring shrine, on the north, was dedicated to Tlaloc, spirit of Earth and water. There were no specifically Mexica connotations on this side; it would have made equal sense elsewhere and in other times (chapters 4 and 5; 4). For the Mexica observed that water lies under the ground; and, like many other Native American peoples, they thought of Earth as an island floating upon water and surrounded by it. Tenochtitlan was a microcosm, then, and the Great Temple a representation of the city itself. Most other communities in the central highlands had the same view of their capitals and their shrines, even though their's were not literally islands (but see plate 25).

For either of the Great Temple's shrines and the pair together, the concept was that they stood in the middle of the world and on a middle plane, the Sun coursing above, like the eagle, by day, and beneath the waters of the underworld by night. It was probably the same for every altepetl's principal temple. Their sites were valued so much that, when enhanced, the new shrine had to stand right above its predecessors. Hence, after successive enlargements, the pyramid enclosed a series of earlier versions of the temple. Archaeologists discovered at the Great Temple that, tearing it down in 1521, the Spanish had not noticed the earlier versions, and that the floor and lower walls of the little temple of the late 1300s are preserved intact, details of its layout and decoration corresponding closely to descriptions of its sixteenth-century successor. The pattern is the same at the Great Temple of Tlatelolco (plate 26). At Cholula, where the mighty pyramid remains, visitors trace the phases of building along a tunnel (plate 28).

Mesoamericans think of life as an energy from the Sun, circulating throughout the world. Hence, standing on a pyramid, priests and other performers were agents of the cosmos (plate 29). Just as the battle fought properly was a rite, so, through its performers, the climax of a rite carried out properly brought people into touch and harmony with 'the gods' for an eternal moment in which the commotion of life was suspended. Again, there is every evidence to suggest that this concept was widespread and ancient. Can a couple of examples make sense of Aztec rites, then?

Sacrifice to Xipe Totec, spirit of new growth, was performed late in the dry season. Prisoners from battles of the previous months were taken up the pyramid to Huitzilopochtli's shrine. There they were flung down, their hearts cut out, and one of their thighs sent to the Tlatoani. The rest of the corpses were shared among the captors' companions and relatives. One prisoner was spared for a while, painted, handed toy weapons and then attacked with real arms. His corpse was skinned and a priest donned the skin to cavort about for the rest of the day until, in the heat, the skin burst to reveal the living man beneath – like corn sprouting from the soil in which the dead were buried, like the people from the bones retrieved by the Feathered Serpent (chapter 1).

Another prisoner, selected for his good looks and wit, was spared for a whole year. He was trained to speak well, to play music, to carry flowers (a habit still sometimes enjoyed by women and men in traditional villages), and then paraded about the city. At the end of the dry season, he was taken to the Tlatoani, dressed with the signs of the omnipotent god Tezcatlipoca, paraded about again, and given four wives. *Then* he was made to throw his accoutrements away and hand gifts and food out to the citizens; and he was taken to a temple in the lake. Climbing the steps there, he broke up and dropped his flute and whistle. At the top, he was flung down and his heart slashed out and held up to the Sun. The prisoner's year acknowledged the seasons, tracing, in his training, the careful cultivation of crops, reflecting, in his glory, the fruits of diligence and, in his death, the deaths of all.

The Aztecs thought of life as a process of complementary values (34). Quetzalcoatl himself, the Feathered Serpent, is the epitome of this dualism. It was thus that they espoused both Toltec and Chichimec identity. They were confident but they also believed that, as time goes round, the world must end, that, as the previous one was flooded, so their's would be destroyed by earthquake – excess of the movement of life.

However, they did not know just when that would happen. It was a source of doubt and worry. Motecuhzoma was apparently preoccupied with it. On the other hand, not only this basic one but all issues of fate could be predicted to some degree by astrologers or by tests such as the Ball Game; and fate could even be manipulated by prayer, ritual and right behaviour. For instance, although postponement was dangerous, the prospects of a child born on an inauspicious day could be improved by waiting to name it on a fortunate one.

The most dramatic expression of these concerns was the New Fire ceremony, conducted at the turn of every cycle of 52 years (last performed in 1507; *28*). All fires were put out at dusk and a

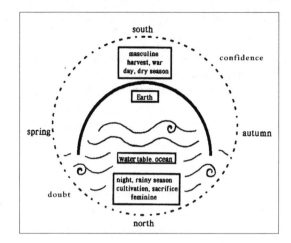

34 Aztec
world-view, Sun
(broken line)
circling Earth

procession made its way to Star Hill, where the heart sacrifice was
performed and the priests kindled fire upon the victim's chest.
The flame was then brought down to the city and the fires relit;
but failure to kindle that light on the Hill would have been a sign
that the Sun was not to rise again. The burden of maintaining the
world is characteristic of the whole round of public rites.

A couple of comparisons may clarify the Aztecs' view on the
world. The Zapotecs distinguished ten principal spirits or pairs of
spirits, each probably associated with one of the 13 numbered days
of the ritual calendar. The spirits' main spheres of influence seem to
have been life and death, illness and medicine, hunting and fishing,
maize and rainfall. Tarascan worship – or the cult approved by the
state – was organized in the same kind of way but the 'pantheon'
was arranged more simply around the spirits of the Sun – the state
deity – the Moon or Venus, and Earth.

Are these religions polytheistic? Analysing the Aztec 'pantheon',
H.B. Nicholson found three main themes: creativity and cosmic
power; rain, water and agricultural fertility; and war and sacrifice.
'Gods' of each implied the others: fertility, for example, is a kind
of creativity, and sacrifice was the work to stimulate that fertility.
Students trying to trace distinct gods are soon baffled by apparently inconsistent invocations to composite spirits. Specific invoca-

tions probably depended on particular requirements; probably, as elsewhere in the world, people did personify spiritual aspects of special concern; and, no doubt, priests commonly recommended well tried formulae while, of course, monthly rites dwelt on particular 'gods'; but, ultimately, as in Hinduism, they were aspects of a single system. The Zapotec spirit of Thirteen, for instance, was considered to be infinite and the creator of everything.

The Aztecs struggled with this: how could movement or life originate from a unitary principle? Thinkers probing the myths of origin worked out that the very first and highest in the cosmos must be a spirit of two complementary values; and yet, with suggestive dualism, poets whispered of attaining harmony by transcending movement between entities:

> I crave flowers that will not perish in my hands!
> Where might I find such lovely flowers, lovely songs?
> Such as I seek, spring does not produce on earth.

OUT OF BALANCE?

The economic crisis of the early 1450s was evidently a turning point. The military strategy was extended and the Great Temple enlarged. These developments are reminiscent of the changes at Teotihuacan in about 300; but, unlike their predecessors, the Aztecs emphasised their local groups, the calpollis, and they intensified the municipal rites.

When Ahuitzotl reconsecrated the Great Temple, in 1487, he summoned the whole citizenry as well as foreign dignitaries to witness the sacrifice of 80,400 captives. This figure is not necessarily to be taken at face value, but it is difficult to escape the implication that at least 20,000 were killed. At the same time, Ahuitzotl made generous gifts, again, to the citizens and also the foreign lords attending (including the Tarascans), pointing out to the latter that the presents were his military booty. As with the Classic Maya, the emphasis was on acquiring – and disposing of – goods and life from abroad.

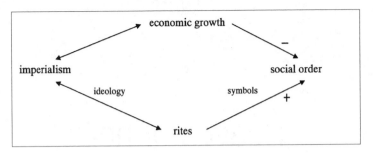

35 The function of public rites in Tenochtitlan? Compare *13*

The Allies' enemies treated captives alike if not in such numbers. Again, like the Aztecs, the Zapotecs and Tarascans, for example, made limited heart sacrifices for regular seasonal ceremonies. Sacrifice was the harvest of battle. Among the Aztecs, military aggression, in turn, was probably driven by economic and political demand in the city; but could the ceremony not have been adapted to turnover? Certainly, it was costly to keep many captives 'fat' for sacrifice. Nezahualcoyotl, philosopher prince, paragon of Toltec virtues, was said to have argued that mass slaughter debased the rite; and, for people, fabled Topiltzin of Tollan wanted to substitute quails, butterflies and rabbits . . .

The Mexica used the 'shock value' of human sacrifice to make a point. It was performed to be witnessed. What was that point, then?

Terror can evoke the power of gods. No doubt the rites were presented as the acme of Huitzilopochtli's principle of assertive action. There are hints that apologists explained them as their barbarian heritage. Perhaps, as E.D. Purdum & J.A. Paredes have suggested, they were like executions of convicts in the USA, to reassure the public that 'society is not out of control after all'; and perhaps they were laid on, like the Roman circus and for the same desperate municipal reason, as entertainment. In 1487, the army's return was carefully marked, like a Roman triumph, by parading the captives through Tenochtitlan's suburbs to the Great Temple. For, so long as the army was on the move and tribute flowed in, the governors could maintain political initiative (*35*).

8

Heaven or hell

Mesoamerica was conquered by soldiers and microbes. Everyone knows how, in Mexico and then Peru, small parties of Conquistadores toppled the Indian empires. The military story and its sequel are full of daring, cunning, cruelty and lust; but the main cause was a series of epidemics over which the Europeans had no more control than their victims.

Its peoples were the greatest asset of their new empire for the Spanish. Yet it is hard, at first, to imagine how any Native societies survived. The losses in Mesoamerica were so heavy that they threatened customary patterns of life, while, at the same time, the Spanish insisted on new ways of work and thought. It had already occurred in the West Indies and it was to recur everywhere else in the Americas. There are regions of South America where the pattern of epidemics, exploitation and evangelization is still being allowed to happen.

Where the Aztecs, favouring their demands for tribute over the requirements of largely independent domestic economies, had reduced some communities to peasantry, the Spanish turned the whole Native world into a peasantry within a couple of generations. Yet, while Indians still vastly outnumbered others, the years from about 1532 to 1545 were something of a golden period; and, by the later seventeenth century, as the colonial economy slumped, many communities had found ways to contain the threats. They had faced doom and they were cheating it; but the Early Colonial period, to about 1650, covered in the present chapter, sowed the seeds of troubles to be recounted in the next.

THE CONQUISTADORES

The Spanish Conquest was part of Europe's expansion around the whole world. The landing of Hernán Cortés and his band on the Gulf coast of Mexico in 1519 was a stage in the colonization that Columbus had begun in 1492.

It was Columbus himself, in 1502, who made first contact with Mesoamericans. In the Gulf of Honduras, he intercepted one of the great canoes that plied to and from Yucatan. The Indians were shocked but, for the Spaniards, other than the intriguing impression of well-clad traders, their humble paddlers and their cargo, there were no direct consequences because the Spanish Main and Cuba seemed more promising. By 1517, however, the Indians and the minerals of Cuba were so depleted that ambitious colonists determined to explore further west. A team with the pilot whom Columbus had taken in 1502 reached Yucatan and survived clashes with the Maya. Another, the next year, confirmed that Yucatan and the Gulf coast promised wealth; and that was the cue for Cortés (*36*).

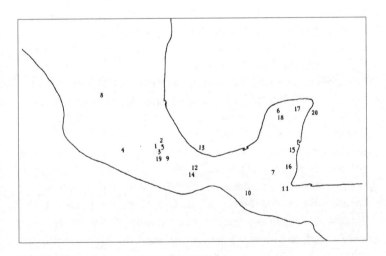

36 The Early Colonial period: 1 Mexico City, Tlalnepantla; 2 Tlaxcala, Zultepec; 3 Cholula; 4 Tzintzuntzan; 5 Puebla City; 6 Mérida; 7 Nojpeten (Tayasal); 8 Zacatecas; 9 Tlayacapan; 10 Momostenango; 11 Sacapulas; 12 Ixtepeji; 13 Veracruz; 14 Mitla; 15 Lamanai; 16 Tipu; 17 Izamal; 18 Oxcutzcab; 19 Chalma; 20 Cozumel

Cortés set off with some 500 followers before the wary governor
of Cuba could gainsay him. Putting in at Cozumel, he was greeted
by the Spanish survivor of a wreck in 1511 who had learnt Yucatec.
Reinforced with this asset, the expedition proceeded until attacked
by the westernmost Maya. In the ensuing parley, Cortés was offered
several women, among them Doña Marina, 'La Malinche', who
spoke both Yucatec and Nahuatl. She completed his linguistic
bridge to the Aztecs.

Meanwhile, word had reached Tenochtitlan and envoys were
sent to intercept Cortés on the Totonac shore. They brought him
the long plumes of the quetzal; and gold. Cortés decided to put
down. There was fighting with the Totonacs. Gathering intelligence about the Aztecs, he learned not only of their cities and of
much more treasure but also of local resentment about the burden
of tribute. He persuaded the Totonacs that he could liberate them.
With a corps of their new allies, the Spanish marched into the
mountains, making first for Tlaxcala. Here, the round of fighting
and treaty was repeated and, reinforced with 6000 Tlaxcaltecs, the
party pressed on. Having terrorized Cholula into acquiescence,
they crossed between the two presiding volcanoes into the Valley
of Mexico. They were awestruck; but, losing no time on tourism,
Cortés took the Tlatoani hostage.

Cortés was set back by news of a force from Cuba sent to arrest
him. Leaving Motecuhzoma guarded under the ferocious Pedro de
Alvarado, he met the posse, fought, and then persuaded them to
join him. By the time that he got back to Tenochtitlan, however,
the Mexica had decided to expel the Spanish, and he had to lead
a desperate retreat to Tlaxcala.

His next entry to the Valley of Mexico was an all-out attack
with nearly 70,000 Native allies. The Mexica appealed to the
Tarascans for help but got short shrift; some of the envoys were
sacrificed. Depending on local attitudes to the Mexica or assess-
ments of the chances, the invaders were welcomed in some towns
and bitterly resisted by others. One startling discovery in 2004
was of a mass grave from the Aztec period at Zultepec: some
of the bones are probably European – all the dead, Native and
foreign, are thought to have been victims of sacrifice. Texcoco

threw its lot in with Cortés. Cutting their way into the city, in 1521, the Spanish were taken aback by the spiteful brutality of the Tlaxcaltecs alongside them. Tlaxcaltec historians, for their part, recorded it as the year in which, aided by some Spanish advisors, they finally prevailed over the Mexica. In 2008, a mass grave was discovered at Tlateloclo, dating from the time of the Conquest and with the bodies laid out in Christian form.

The Great Temple and the other shrines were torn down, and Mexico City began to rise upon the ruins (plate 26). Spanish colonists started to stream in. They marked the centre off and forbade Indians to live among them there. At the same time, Cortés sent parties out to claim the surrounding territories and their peoples. Like the Aztecs and most other imperialists, the Spanish sought to assert themselves through the local lords. Many accepted Spanish authority. Tlaxcaltec collaboration was rewarded, for a while, with semi-autonomy in their homeland – which probably attracted refugees from surrounding districts. For security, Tlaxcaltecs and some Otomís were settled in places as colonists. By the end of the century, they found themselves in northern Mexico, and the Tlaxcaltecs spread as far as New Mexico and Texas. Again, some Tlaxcaltec historians regarded these ventures as autonomous. Effectively extending Mesoamerican language, social life and farming, their settlements in northern Mexico remained distinctive for at least two centuries.

The Tarascan king was retained as a client until 1530 but, by then, diseases, colonists and missionaries had undermined his realm. Next, the Spanish invaded the populous region to the west and north-west but, since political organization here was less centralized, conquest proved more difficult and the invaders were pinned down in the Mixton War (1541-2). Many people fled for the hills where they evaded the Europeans for the best part of two centuries. The Huichols rose repeatedly during the early 1600s. Once, they were encouraged by the prophecy that martyrs would return to life after three days (note the Christian influence). The northern Zapotecs too resisted vicious attacks intermittently until the 1550s, and their Mixe neighbours fought back until 1570.

It took many years to conquer the Maya. The mountains were invaded in 1523. The Zinacantecos pitched in to attack their neighbours, the Chamulas. The Kaqchikels joined Alvarado against the K'ich'es, and the Tz'utujils and then the Pipils too; but they stopped collaborating when he tried to extort tribute and labour from them as well as levying troops. Honduras was invaded in 1524-6 but resistance there did not end until 1536. Yucatan's turn came in 1527-8 but not until 1542 could the Conquistadores lay the foundations of their provincial capital, Mérida, over the rubble of Tiho. The last organized resistance in Yucatan broke out in 1546-7, when every link to the Spanish was purged, collaborators for sure, and dogs and cats and plants.

Between Yucatan and the mountains, the forests proved intractable and protected refugees from the north and probably the south too. The heartland of the Classic Maya has continued to nurture resistance to surrounding regimes; but, finally, in 1697 – after 150 years – the last town, Nojpeten, did capitulate. The tiny population of Lakandons remained independent until long into the 1900s.

THE VIRUSES AND BACTERIA

The Europeans and their African slaves brought with them an invisible cargo of infections. Although familiar with these conditions, they hardly understood them and, hence, could do little to contain them. The invaders themselves often succumbed, but their mortality was negligible by comparison.

Epidemics almost ended Mesoamerica by 1650; but a couple of interpretive problems hinder analysis of the process. First, reports of the time often leave doubt as to which conditions were at work. Secondly, it is very difficult to assess the numbers killed by the first epidemics; and that is important, in turn, for assessing the social history of the first five generations of the Colonial period. For, while the records permit reasonably reliable estimates of population once Spanish administration was in place, historians disagree as to the total on the eve of the Conquest. Thirdly, the losses were caused not only by disease but also by the attendant social and economic disruption; and the decline also owed to demoralized

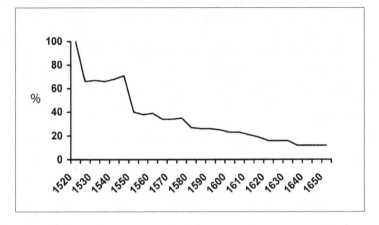

37 The collapse of population 1520-1650

'drop outs' who joined the growing population of mixed race (compare chapter 9). By how much, then, did population decline? Setting controversially high and low estimates aside, it transpires that the loss was some 90 per cent from 1520 to 1650 (37).

What does this stunning figure mean? It takes no account of the experiences of particular generations, let alone particular communities. It is probably true of Central and much of southern Mexico; but, while the Maya may have survived at the rate of almost 20 per cent in parts of the highlands and, before 1648, in Yucatan, some coastal populations were practically extinguished. The nadir was probably a generation before 1650 in Central Mexico and perhaps rather later in the north. The pattern of decline explains much of the history to that point. It happened in steps.

First came smallpox. The chart (37) shows a conservative estimate of its toll. The epidemic broke out in Tlaxcala while Cortés was regrouping there, and then became his vanguard: by the time that he got back to Tenochtitlan, the defenders were already decimated. The young and the old died in much greater numbers than others. The virus probably thrived especially in the cooler and drier conditions of the mountains, where the biggest populations lived. Yet it seems to have reached the Maya even before Tlaxcala, three years ahead of the first major Spanish expedition.

The same epidemic probably reached the Incas, well before the Conquistadores.

Then came measles, which ravaged Cuba in 1529 and seems to have struck Mexico (and Florida) two years later. Possibly in conjunction with other illnesses, the infection reached the highland Maya in 1532 and the Gulf of California a year later. By now too, the Gulf of Mexico coast had succumbed to malaria.

The third major epidemic started in 1545. It was probably typhus. It raged for three years. Older survivors of the first smallpox succumbed in high numbers; and younger children proved susceptible too. The toll from this one may have been the worst of them all.

In 1550, mumps broke out. Influenza seems to have struck in 1558-9, probably derived from an epidemic in Europe, and this outbreak was apparently compounded by other diseases. Both smallpox and measles spread again in 1563-4.

The last major scourges were from 1576 to 1580 and in 1595-6. They included typhus, smallpox, measles and possibly bubonic plague. Often, survivors of one contagion were too weak to withstand the next.

There were serious outbreaks of smallpox and measles in Central and western Mexico in 1615-7. Typhus struck Guatemala in 1607-8 and spread from Central Mexico to terrible effect in 1631-2. Plague was probably at large too. Many lesser outbreaks of various diseases occurred and local disasters were numberless. In the late 1640s, yellow fever took hold in the Caribbean and hit the eastern lowlands and Gulf Coast of Mexico, this one afflicting all races alike.

Traditional treatments failed or even exacerbated the conditions. Missionaries claimed credit for saving some people in 1531 with their own methods of hygiene. Nor, certainly, did diseases account directly and solely for the total toll. Some Native treatments were inappropriate. Sometimes, frightened villagers fled as the first fell ill, and an unknown number of orphans and elderly, perhaps unafflicted, died of neglect. Some of the mortality was attributed to starvation owing to interruption of the heavy daily task of preparing maize. Yet more basic was disruption of farm tasks, from clearing the fields to storing the harvest (9). Nor can it be doubted that the arbitrary dislocation of ordinary life and the horror of some of the symptoms sapped the will to live.

Diseases continued to strike. There was a devastating epidemic in 1736-9, probably typhus. Yet, of course, such experience was common the world over. From the mid seventeenth century, the Native population as a whole reached equilibrium by virtue of immunities.

GOVERNMENT

For most of the colonists, labour was the critical resource, not only as an economic asset but also for its connotations of social standing. The Crown took a paternal attitude to the Indians; and likewise the Church, stirred by its evangelic opportunities. The problem for each was as to how the Indians should be organized.

For Columbus, appraising that party off Honduras, Cortés, observing the Totonacs' attitudes to their own lords and the Mexica, and for every Conquistador thereafter, the key was Native organization. In effect, the Crown concurred that, first, it should simply replace the top tier in order to inherit the rest intact; and, on that basis, it determined to ensure justice for both colonists and Natives.

'Native lords' (caciques, as the Spanish sometimes called them too, adapting a Caribbean word) were manipulated to serve the conquerors. Hence the boundaries and the names of many ancient communities were preserved. Although the dynasts of the Triple Alliance complained that their authority was reduced too much, members of the Mexica royal family were even granted Spanish privileges. 25 years after the Conquest, most surviving nobles retained most of their prerogatives, some were marrying Spaniards and buying into the new economy, and a few still ranked among Mexico's wealthiest. It probably benefited some dependent communities, which seem to have valued their lords as buffers against the colonists. Yet, by lopping off the top tier of Native authority, the government sundered communities from each other, neutralizing that play of alliance and subordination which had been the whole life of politics. Increasingly, moreover, nobles from one district were appointed, arbitrarily in the Native view, to offices elsewhere.

However, the epidemic of 1545-8 diminished both the nobles' economic base and their importance for either the Spanish or the Indians. From the 1550s, along with attempts to recalculate tribute on the basis of maize and money, the government progressively reduced the amount and variety of nobles' dues and curtailed their privileges. Some compensated with rents from their private estates or by enterprise; and they fared better in a few remoter parts, whether with substantial wealth, as some Zapotecs and Mixtecs, or just in relative affluence, as in Yucatan.

One of the main problems was that the Colonial government was slow to adjust its calculations of tax to the decline of population. To some extent, the difficulty was circumvented by progressively substituting personal taxes for collective tribute. Yet that further weakened distinctions between lords and commoners – the same effect as that found by archaeologists tracing the economic impact of the Aztecs. On the other hand, collection of the dues remained the responsibility of local political leaders who often respected ranking colleagues' claims to exemption and enriched themselves by adding their own charges.

In the mid 1500s, local government was progressively reformed by introducing a Spanish pattern of ranked but rotating municipal offices, the cabildo. It tended to diminish noble power somewhat; but, in many towns, the new officers discovered that the duties were – and are – so time consuming that they called them 'cargos', burdens. Yet, both in Morelos and in Yucatan, the offices were adapted to local custom. Again perhaps reminiscent of the paired motifs in Oaxaca's Early Formative cemeteries, the Mixe villages, northeast of Mitla, are arranged in two parts for taking turns to bear the cargos. At the same time, municipal estates were defined and guaranteed against colonists' depredations and the communities were made to establish collective funds. Thus was created a lattice of 'Indian republics' (repúblicas de indios).

Alongside civilian government, the church laid parishes out. They were the basis for tithes and various other dues; and some bishops became notorious for special levies. The parishes were also the base to which, from the mid 1500s, was attached a version of the European cofradías, lay brotherhoods. They seem to have developed at least as strongly among the Maya as in the west, and they have lasted among them more strongly too. Ostensibly clubs for celebrating particular cults or ensuring performance of certain rites, the cofradías were probably intended to compensate priests for dwindling income from declining congregations. Yet, in the 1600s, many cofradías took on a life of their own with corporate property and a hierarchy of offices. Undertaken a year at a time, these too are commonly called cargos because they entail sponsorship of processions, dances and feasts – burdens which resemble ancient chiefly duties.

Since the cofradías came to involve many or most of the men of a community (and, in parts, some of the women), their political importance became at least as great as the cabildos'. Indeed, although the emphasis on one or the other varied – and varies – from region to region, the two hierarchies commonly formed a 'ladder' up which men rose through positions alternately in one and the other. One Zapotec claim stated that (like Eight Deer of old) the ancestors had acquired authority from afar, from Mexico City and Spain. The favours and debts entailed were once thought to hold societies together in conformity and equality but study of achievers has revealed that, among the K'ich'e up to the mid 1700s, leadership tended to remain with particular families, and that, in Yucatan, the residual nobility managed to retain leadership until late that century.

A new if modest Native elite developed in most districts. From the mid 1500s to the nineteenth century, moreover, many local leaders succeeded in exploiting the law to obtain enhanced status for their communities or themselves. Ploys of the same kind were common under the Aztec yoke, and probably just as bitter; but while, formerly, they often resulted in punitive tribute all round, now it was the courts' ponderous procedure that made the game so expensive.

WORK

Local administration provided a framework for the colonists to exploit Indian labour but more specific mechanisms were needed for recruiting and directing gangs. The measures ranged from adaptions of traditional Native institutions to force. Private management at the outset was gradually superseded by public regulation which gave way, in turn, to manipulation by private contract.

When the Spanish discovered, in Central Mexico, that adult men were used to making themselves available, in turns, for local public works, they seized on the custom. Indeed, it is still maintained by some rural councils and known by an old Nahuatl term, tequio or coatequitl, tribute snake. Owing to comparatively high survival of the first epidemic among younger adults, labour was plentiful from 1521 to 1545. However, the exactions for building Mexico City, Puebla City and elsewhere were soon much resented. Nor is tequio regarded with great respect or affection today.

Up to the mid 1500s, the Spaniards' principal means of exploitation was encomienda, trusteeship. It was conceived as a reward for service in conquests. Beneficiaries expected to receive a community or group of communities, usually defined by Native lordships, in return for providing priests. The arrangement was treated as a form of the tributes due to the lords in Aztec days.

Of course, it failed: the Indians were abused, Tarascans, for example, made to travel away to mines; the Church protested about both the cruelty and failure to fulfil the missionary condition; the Crown agreed that cruelty had to be stopped, it was embarrassed by officials' abuses, and it was wary of the implications of large populations in private hands; and the beneficiaries themselves complained as the value of their grants declined with falling population – notably during 1545-8 (37). Yet encomiendas persisted in remoter regions into the eighteenth century.

In 1549, a labour tax or corvée was introduced, repartimiento (division or assignment). There was no pastoral condition and the number of workers was stipulated; but hours were stipulated too, and wages. Cabildos could deploy whom they wished but beneficiaries were assured of a certain number of workers, and the increasing number of colonists and range of tasks could be provided for. Various types of repartimiento were developed. After the epidemics of the late 1570s, some of the regulations were circumvented, leaving workers less time to maintain their own fields.

In the mountains of northern Oaxaca, extortion of cotton cloth and dye (cochineal) continued, with this effect, well into the 1700s.

Abuses proliferated in remoter districts but the most notorious repartimientos were those for draining the lake around Mexico City in 1555-6 and during the 1600s and 1700s. Otherwise, repartimiento was progressively phased out in Mexico, in the later sixteenth century and the early seventeenth, in favour of unregulated wage labour. Central America witnessed the same tendency but repartimiento continued there into the following century.

From the later 1500s, the main sector of growth in the money economy was agriculture. Demand for wheat and meat rose with the growth of European and mixed populations. It was concentrated not only in the highland districts long relatively densely populated but also, from about 1550, in the mining zone of Zacatecas, which needed leather equipment as well as food. There was also a big market for leather and textiles in Spain. The country between the Valley of Mexico and Zacatecas was suited to both pastoral and arable farming and, once Chichimec raids were curtailed by catching culprits and settling Tarascans and Otomís, the region began to boom. As the supply of labour dwindled, colonists, Native nobles and the Church alike invested in farms and ranches, haciendas, and in plantations, creating many permanent and temporary jobs. The wages were mean but attractive to men caught in the dilemmas of repartimiento and the cargos; and, for many, they were the only way to accumulate enough cash for tributary and ecclesiastical dues. However, the haciendas trapped workers by indebting them with advances on wages (debt peonage).

There were alternatives. Partly in response to low food prices during the 1540s and '50s and to the efforts of Mexico City to control the cost of grain, many rural and suburban people took up trade. The Mixtecs developed a booming silk industry. Low wages and plentiful labour favoured the ancient use of men for haulage. Even as population fell, the colonial economy grew and imperial freight across Mexico from Peru and the Philippines increased, so mule trains became more common. Many Indians set up as hauliers.

Some fleeing the countryside found work as servants. The friaries employed large retinues. The conditions were poor but worse off were those who found themselves in factories and wool mills (obrajes). The government tried to prohibit repartimiento there but the courts did send convicts and orphans. Then there was the mining. Mines were sunk in many districts but the silver mines of Zacatecas were much the biggest and most notorious.

There was slavery too at first. In the 1520s, Huastecs were carried off to replace Native labour lost in the Caribbean. Indians from Nicaragua were imported to Guatemala. Until the frontier zone was brought within the pale of imperial justice, Chichimecs were enslaved. Where Native population fell too far – along the Gulf coast, for example – Africans were imported.

The colonial economy cleft people from their traditions. Nahuatl incorporated many more Spanish nouns once repartimiento began. One of the most conservative features was food: there was widespread adherence to maize and beans and antipathy to wheat. Various fruits were adopted and, during the early boom in herding, meat may have been eaten although later, other than chicken at festivals, it disappeared from most people's diet. However, the less that they stayed in their villages, working their own land, the weaker became the Indian economy and the more they took on the new culture. The less that they lived as peasants, the more they became proletarians.

LAND

Mesoamerica's imperial value changed with the collapse of population. If the pressure, during the first 60 years, was on the Indians' labour, thereafter it was on their land.

With fewer to feed or to work, Indian communities gradually abandoned outlying fields. To European eyes, vacant countryside was 'waste', with both economic implications and moral connotations. Although government policy respected well-founded Native claims, colonists set about creating estates which progressively absorbed the unused land.

Of the various conflicts ensuing, the commonest were about herds. The Spanish could not have replaced the Indians quickly enough but that the livestock took to the grass and shrubs as the diseases to the people. They constantly encroached upon the remaining Indian fields. They drank irrigation water and polluted it. Erosion of soil in the Valley of Mexico and in Otomí country, to the north, was exacerbated by grazing on the slopes. In Central Mexico, the herds reached parity with the Indians by about 1575 and outnumbered them tenfold by 1620. The mountain Mixtecs and some of the mountain Maya became excellent sheep farmers but their herds too had caused erosion by the later 1700s.

As colonial demand increased, the main device for releasing land was to gather Indians in new towns – a sort of reservations. This strategy of congregación or reducción originated in the West Indies and was later to develop on a larger scale in South America. Most of the congregaciones were established in the 1550s and 1593-1605 (37). To be sure, one problem was that, in the countryside, the epidemics left many survivors isolated and helpless. Government and church agreed that administration, inculcation of civic virtues

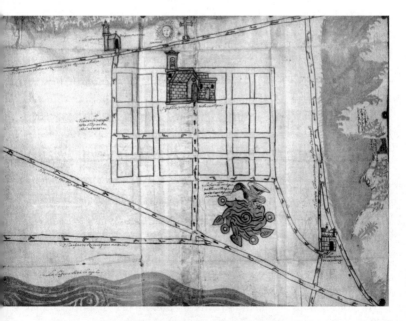

38 Model town: Chicoalapan (near Mexico City) depicted by a Nahua in about 1579 (typical renditions of routes, lake, at bottom, and woody hills, at right)

and cure of souls alike would improve in towns laid out on grids around church and town hall at a central plaza (*38*). The Mixes evaded the reform, while, around Momostenango and apparently at Tlayacapan, the distribution of shrines and the testimony of oral tradition reveal how the Indians created new spiritual landscapes according to ancient principles of social identity. Not all of the towns worked, however. One group of new settlements south of Mexico City dispersed within two or three generations. Where catchments were defined without regard to earlier settlement patterns, ethnicity or language, some of the towns proved unworkable. Tlalnepantla, 'place in between', split, eventually, into its Tepanec and Otomí components. In time honoured fashion, Sacapulas preserved its distinctions by segmenting. Worse than impractical, however, many of the towns were traps where contagion thrived. Nor could the policy work where the economy required dispersal, as in the Huichols' rugged country.

CHRISTIANITY

'The gods are dead, let us die', lamented the Mexica. Yet the first main Christian missions seemed to save them. Spanish imperialism had begun as a crusade against the Moors and it bore its Christian commitment to Mesoamerica and beyond. The walk from Veracruz to Mexico City by 12 thin, unarmed, unshod and bare-headed Franciscan friars in 1524 caused a sensation. Ostensive and practical, it was typical of their order's method. Amidst the maelstrom of conquest and disease, the message of love and hope was greeted with fervour.

The key monuments of the early Colonial period are churches. They were built atop or beside ancient religious sites such as the main temples in Tenochtitlan and Tlatelolco, Cholula or Mitla (plates 26 and 28). Lamanai, Belize, used to be called Indian Church for the building perched on one of the pyramids there. Many other churches probably stand over the foundations of temples. In some, walls reveal fragments of prehispanic masonry. Since there were not enough friars to replace the Native priests, the first churches were immense timber halls. Then 'open chapels' were built, with big yards laid out for the multitudes. In less populous areas, the churches were modest. A small one has been investigated by archaeologists at Tipu, replete with its cemetery. Churches, other public buildings and monasteries of the period look European but the Native handiwork can be detected in the motifs, arrangement and technique of carved or painted ornament. Featherworkers' talents were turned to images and vestments.

Like the temporal conquerors, the friars exploited Native organization by concentrating, first, on schooling the nobles. Mass baptisms of their people followed. The most obvious Indian rites were quickly stopped, and the libraries burnt on the assumption that the whole literature was corrupt. Nahuatl was transcribed in the Latin alphabet and 'A Christian doctrine' printed in the late 1520s. The friars put much store on teaching children too. It is telling, however, that the rate of attendance at church fell, in the Valley of Mexico, from the 1550s and '60s, probably owing partly to loss of the nobles' cohesive influence; and where, in Tlaxcala, they enjoyed more autonomy, conversion was comparatively weak during the early Colonial period. Equally, the Tz'utujils, whose resistance to the Conquistadores had been comparatively brief, were blessed with fewer priests than their stubborner neighbours.

The friars soon discovered how to adapt traditional holidays, processions and dances. The ancient Day of the Dead was fused with All Souls', and is still celebrated avidly in Mexico. Many villages preserve festival dances evidently taught or influenced by the missionaries. The best known are versions of 'Moors and Christians'. Less affected by missionaries, perhaps, the forms of many others preserve prehispanic symbols. The friars devised didactic plays too. One production at Tlatelolco, in 1533, is said to have involved 800 actors and musicians and spectators as numerous as the crowds at market there 14 years before!

At the same time, Vasco de Quiroga set up communities near Mexico City and Tzintzuntzan inspired by Thomas More's 'Utopia'. Four or five years later, Bartolomé de las Casas, former colonist turned campaigner for peaceful conversion, established a model community, Verapaz, among the K'eq'chi and Pokomchi, in Guatemala. Both of these experiments were closed to Spaniards at first.

The response was creative too. Like their predecessors before the Spanish Conquest, Native staff appointed to run churches from week to week took their duties seriously. For didactic or pragmatic reasons, many missionaries tolerated assimilation of saints with ancient cults. Families depleted and sundered by the epidemics took up Spanish customs – notably godparenthood (compadrazgo) and cofradías – as forms of social and economic security. Pilgrimages developed. During the 1530s began slowly the greatest of them, that of the Virgin of Guadalupe. There was, at first, an implication that She cares especially for the Indians, and the authorities worried too that the site of Her apparition outside Mexico City, had been an Aztec shrine. Chalma almost certainly has such a pedigree (plate 30). At Izamal, the Church was quick to adopt and adapt an ancient shrine by fitting it up grandly.

By the 1540s, in the Valley of Mexico, many Nahuas denied that they owed anything to the abominated Aztecs. The rate of culture change varied with intensity of exposure to the colonists and with the lords' influence over their people; but how much did the quality of culture alter?

Segregation hampered assimilation even in cities; and the countryside proved obdurate. The missionary effort was weakened by the Church's reluctance to ordain Indians; and many priests were afraid to antagonize their flocks. Folk Catholicism thrived among the cofradías. The saints were popular, and still are, their images carefully clad in garments, as were prehispanic statues. Jesus was commonly ranked among them; and, for many purposes, there He remains. Saints were – and are – commonly worshipped as community patrons, so that the parish church was a substitute for the old temple. However, in the eighteenth century, the elderly of Huitzilopochco, near Mexico City, refused to let stone be robbed for their church from the ruins of the Aztec temple, nearby, on the grounds that there lay the town's 'strength'.

Syncretism developed too, melding of beliefs. In places, during the 1500s, pagan fetishes were discovered buried in churches. Today, in southern Mesoamerica, Jesus is commonly associated with the Sun, and, alongside the saints, the dreaded Earth Lord (now imagined as a Spanish speaker) is still widely respected.

No orthodox Christian ideas of the soul and its links with God can accommodate such combinations and conflations of spirits. Study of church archives and of contemporary village life has shown something of how they have lasted to this day. A survey of rural south-central Mexico in about 1617-29 discovered extensive use of pagan prayers, fetishes, minor sacrifices and drugs by farmers, weather magicians, healers, midwives and diviners. It also heard reports of sorcery. Much of it based on the ancient sacred calendar, terminology and rites were little changed; and they still flourish in many parts of the countryside. Although aware of priests' disapproval, many practitioners did not think that it precluded Christianity. Nor do they now. For it is propitiatory, investigatory and devoted to particular material ends, a skill which the missionaries had overlooked.

Recent thinking among the K'ich'e Maya probably illustrates an ancient principle. Against the image of a remoter Holy Trinity, they posit God as a spirit embracing all of the saints, including their images in the church, while 'the world' is thought to comprise the sacred mountains, the parish altar and the cemetery, and ancestors make up a third element. Dr Tedlock contrasts 'This ... view ... in which dualities complement rather than clash with one another' to the orthodox 'analytic' distinction between domains of good and evil.

Different from syncretism, perhaps, and simpler, is the simultaneous maintenance of both traditional religion and Christianity ('compartmentalization'). The Huichols, for example, respect both saints and 'Our Grandparents', fire and Sun, 'Mother Earth', 'Our Aunts', rain and sea, and 'Our Brothers', maize and peyote, their ritual hallucinogen. In 1562, boys in Oxcutzcab led friars to a collection of idols in a cave. The ensuing inquisition tortured more than 4500 people, killing 158. It heard that a human sacrifice had been performed in a church (presumably not just naive syncretism). Combinations of belief are more common in remoter districts but a similar 'scandal' was exposed in the Valley of Mexico as late as 1803. Sometimes, in desperation, ancient spirits were invoked during plagues.

There was rejection too. At least one village in the mountains south of Mexico City fled the missionaries; and so did those

Zapotecs of Ixtepeji who had had trouble in sorting out their tributes even before the Spanish Conquest.

By the third quarter of the 1500s, priests' daily experience was that conversion had been superficial. Confusion about the Christian mysteries was widespread: to confessors working in Nahuatl, people described themselves mournfully as 'nepantla', in between. Worse was some of the evidence of daily morale: alcoholism was rife by the 1540s; it was reported that conception had declined among the Tz'utujils and that abortion was common in northern Oaxaca.

9

Resurgence

Immunities to the new diseases began to develop during the seventeenth century. Population stabilized; then numbers began slowly to recover; vaccination has reduced mortality sharply since the later 1880s; and, since 1940, several regions have experienced steep growth. In Guatemala, Indian population has more than doubled since 1950. Yet, ever since the eighteenth century, the Indians have been hemmed in by White and mestizo (mixed) populations growing even more. Expressed in social, political, economic and religious issues, the key consequence was struggle for land (*39* and *40*). The vital unit for the Indians has been the village community.

Every feature of Native culture has been adapted more or less, since the Spanish Conquest. Survival of language is probably the most effective guarantee of substantial local continuity but not all aspects of tradition have necessarily changed in the same degree. Like Archaic life after 2000 BC, old ways persisted in 'refugia', remote from 'development'; but, already in the eighteenth century, custom was a dubious index of heritage. In Yucatan, poorer Spaniards were marrying into leading Maya families; and, even near Mexico City, there were villages where non-Indians found themselves living as Mesoamericans.

Native societies are flourishing again in parts of Mexico and Guatemala, as in some other regions of the Americas, but their conditions are quite unlike those before the Conquest. Owing to economic change and, latterly, to schooling and Christian missions, the sense of identity is fraught; and confrontation with outsiders has made Indians keenly aware of their own traditions. Stand-off with the authorities in Chiapas has become a symbol the world over of grass-roots challenge to globalisation.

Prof. Vogt was once told a story from Zinacantan that expresses both ancient tradition and impacts of Colonial and more recent history. Once upon a time, it goes, Saint Sebastian was a captain. His general had two daughters and wanted him to marry one of them but Sebastian refused. So the general took him off to a rocky place in the woods by the Oaxaca coast and tied him to a tree. The woodlanders tried to kill Sebastian: two jaguars tried, two toucans, a couple of wild people (a man and a woman, the one senior, the other his junior), some demons, and two Lakandons who shot arrows at him because he was a Spanish-speaker, not indigenous (they hated those people and wanted to kill all of them); but none could kill Sebastian. So the general sent soldiers with guns; but they failed too. The general himself came back. He heard a traditional ceremonial drum there. Again he asked Sebastian to marry one of his daughters; Sebastian replied not. So the general assaulted him, first with an ordinary lance and then with a massive one of gold and silver; but Sebastian could not be killed. Next day, a carter heard the drum and found Sebastian; and he also found a book which explained that Sebastian wanted to leave, although his brother and sister, who had come to help him, preferred to stay. The man consulted his comrades; and onto the cart they loaded Sebastian, his drum and his lances, and brought him to Zinacantan. There, the gods of the sky's four corners built Sebastian a church. When, later, the government ordered the destruction of churches and saints, Sebastian and his kit were dispersed and hidden. The repression passed and Sebastian was reinstated but his effects remained dispersed. One day, the two brothers responsible for the drum argued; and the drum vanished. After nearly a year, a shaman found it. One of the brothers insisted on keeping it; but no-one is sure now whether his drum really is the old one.

Were the Indians passive victims or did they help to steer the course of events? As racial boundaries blurred in people of mixed ancestry and in urban 'melting pots', was Indian identity maintained by village conservatives? Or was it merely a symbol of social and economic marginality imposed on indigenous people by the surrounding political and economic system? Will Mesoamerica endure?

STATE AND CHURCH

To understand the period since 1650, it is necessary to recognize the roles both of governments and of religious organizations. A shift of government policy from paternalism to liberalism tended to expose the separated Indian communities to 'global' economic currents. At the same time, missionaries penetrated deeper.

After two centuries of falling population and corruption in the Americas, and of inefficiency in Spain, the Crown determined to improve conditions through the so-called Bourbon Reforms. They sprang from a vision for development through an open market. Attempts to increase local revenue and to combat abuses among collectors, both hispanic and Indian, began in the 1770s. The provision for community chests was repealed. After 15 or 20 years, the new administration filtered down to villagers. In remoter districts, officials enforced labour law against mestizos' abuses. In Central Mexico, on the other hand, they tried to promote schooling in Spanish and to divert cofradías' funds to that end; and they started

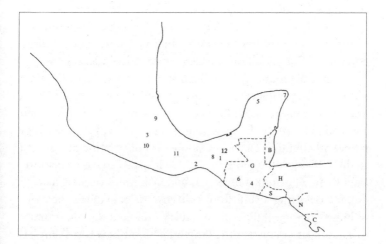

39 The Republican period: Mexico; B Belize; G Guatemala; H Honduras; S El Salvador; N Nicaragua; C Costa Rica; 1 San Cristóbal de las Casas, Zinacantan; 2 Juchitán; 3 Mexico City; 4 Guatemala City; 5 Mérida; 6 Momostenango; 7 Cancun; 8 Tuxtla Gutiérrez; 9 Huejutla; 10 Tepoztlán; 11 Ixtepeji; 12 Ocosingo

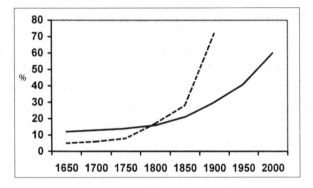

40 Recovery of Indian population 1650-2000 (% of number in
1519) against growth of others' (broken line; estimates)

to insist that public documents should be in Spanish, not Nahuatl.
At the same time, indigenous leaders adopted Native surnames.

Yet, by 1810, when started the struggle for Mexican independence,
so little had changed that the nationalist movement included a call
to ensure greater autonomy for Indians. In Guatemala, the K'ich'es
contributed to the campaign for independence by trying to restore
their own kingdom. These hopes came to naught, however. The
new republics were less tolerant of Indian custom. The Mexican
government barred Native languages from official transactions.

The liberal programme was maintained in Mexico, culminating,
in 1856, with complete abolition, by President Juárez (a Zapotec),
of corporate property. With an eye particularly to the Church, and
also cofradías' assets, the reasoning was that individuals look after
property better than can corporations (a familiar principle, applied
to the Indians in the USA 30 years later or, indeed, earlier, to the
English in England). Thereafter, cofradías were termed mayor-
domías, reflecting a shift from collective to individual (the may-
ordomo's) responsibility. Some leaders exploited the opportunity
to consolidate their wealth; and competition between them has
stimulated more generous sponsorship. However, the obligations
forced many with fewer resources to seek additional work outside
the community or to 'drop out' altogether. Needless to say, much
land fell into non-Indian hands; and the incoming population

infiltrated civic offices. As the national economy was developed, at the turn of the century, the Maya, particularly, in southern Mexico, were forced into work on lowland lumber and rubber groves. In 1917, collective estates were reinstituted, although most municipalities had to wait for President Cárdenas to enforce the measure, in the 1930s. That eased the shortage of land for a generation. In 1948, the National Indigenist Institute (INI) was established to provide for education, health and economic development among Native groups but, like similar measures elsewhere in the world, this programme has encouraged integration at the expense of local tradition. Since the 1970s, however, the government has claimed to espouse multiculturalism and, in 1998, books in 33 Native languages were distributed to schools.

The experience elsewhere was different. Since the plantation economy, with its demands on land and labour, is more important in Central America, there were fewer concessions.

In Guatemala, the Maya remained in the majority but, despite attempts to relieve social and economic disadvantage, in the 1830s and '40s and mid 1900s, dominant political and economic interests ensured continuing stalemate. In the 1870s and '80s, the government forced communities to divert labour to the developing coffee industry and to sell common land. From the 1960s, the situation was complicated by communist insurgency. By then, the Maya were especially susceptible: the pressure on their resources was acuter than ever; many of their local leaders were politicians rather than traditional ritual authorities; higher literacy aided dissemination of propaganda; and, equally, missionaries were encouraging criticism of material conditions. In 1978, the government's attempt to overcome Indian ambivalence by force precipitated ethnic war.

The dilemmas of development were acutest in El Salvador, where, in the 1930s, most Indians abandoned most of their more obvious signs of ethnicity, including both dress and language, in order to avoid harassment. By contrast, in Belize, although the Maya were affected by successive developments of logging and sugar plantations in the nineteenth century, and, in the 1920s, a boom in collecting 'chicle' during the rainy season – for chewing gum – land for subsistence was plentiful and conflict rare.

During the seventeenth and eighteenth centuries, alongside the government's efforts to overcome the Indians' isolation, the Church, less cautious than before, determined repeatedly to draw them more tightly around the priesthood and to curtail idolatry. Several times, notably in Central Mexico during the later 1700s, the response was a movement for rites and prayers to be performed independently of Whites and mestizos. Some formed around charismatic figures or men attributed with supernatural powers. Movements of this type (known as revitalization) still spring up.

In the later 1700s, the Church, like the government, sought to enhance its revenues by appropriating cofradías' assets. From then if not before, the modesty with which men tried – and try – to avoid their turns in office was not feigned, for to acquit themselves respectably in sponsorship, most had to borrow in cash or kind. Ironically, the Church's strategy was criticized by the civil authorities over the next hundred years because it further impaired local communities' capacity to yield civil dues. In the late nineteenth century, Protestant missions began to infiltrate. They found – and still find – willing ears among men and women frustrated by the social, political and economic demands of the cargos. Local leaders soon recognized the challenge not only to customary worship and festivals but also to the pattern of political authority which partly depended on the cargos. In the mid 1900s, the Catholic church launched a fresh campaign of its own, Catholic Action, intended to overcome 'folk Catholicism', this time by recruiting local catechists. Both movements cleft many villages. Yet Catholic and Protestant missionaries cooperated regularly to support the Maya during the war in Guatemala, in the 1980s; and, since then, the Church has coped with the spiritual and political aftermath in various ways, some defying the government. In general, the evidence shows that the ritual tradition of the Colonial era – the 'costumbres', customs – is finally waning in the present generation.

POLITICAL OPTIONS

From the later 1700s, one consequence of rising population was a tendency for local communities to split into separate groups and, where possible, to found new settlements. It was an ancient principle that preserved the scale of social and political life.

Since the seventeenth century, by the same token, a common response to encroachment and interference was to maintain the caution and secrecy that had grown in regard to all outsiders. Sacred places, time and sacrifice remain vital symbols. Communities guarded their land jealously against non-Indians and other Indians alike. At the same time, they insisted on participation in the round of civil and religious duties. The strategy proved effective for the coherence of the group but frustrating for particular families. As much as a day of men's work each week was – and is – given over to cargos and communal work (tequio), while food to almost the same value for a whole family may have been given away in formal exchanges of favours. The old problem of avoidance and 'dropping out' remains. Eric Wolf's notion of 'closed corporate communities' may be too simple but it does capture something of the experience. Laura Nader discovered a 'harmony ideology' among Zapotecs, whereby local disputes are muffled so as to avoid intrusion by officials. Similar tactics developed among Native villages in New Mexico and Arizona.

Closing up was not feasible everywhere. The 1700s saw an unusual pattern of 'vagrants' in western Mexico: Mesoamericans without villages of their own, descendants, no doubt, of Early Colonial directed migration, they retained features of culture distinctive, presumably, relative to a mestizo population that was still small. In Chiapas, on the other hand, Mam and Tojolabal Maya succumbed to the pressure for agricultural development: by the later 1800s, they were dispersed and, by the mid 1900s, they had lost most obvious signs of ethnicity. Yet the Mams preserved traditional practices in church and village hall ('compartmentalizing' their identity). The Tojolabals developed regional networks for fiestas and, in the late 1980s, they formed, in effect, a local government of their own.

On the other hand, as earlier in the Colonial period, leaders are now using constitutional means for making their claims to resources and justice. The tactic was encouraged, during the 1970s, by the Mexican government, which regarded it as a means of control but organizations such as the Mazahua Native Movement, in Central

Mexico, began to develop more independently. In 1974, the Bishop of San Cristóbal convened a congress for the Indians of Chiapas; and, in 1977, a Mexican Native American congress was held. In 1980-2 and again in 1989, an alliance of Zapotec and other radical politicians took municipal power in Juchitán. Activists in Guatemala City have been promoting recognition of Maya tradition since the mid 1970s and, in 2000, one was appointed to the national government.

The sense of identity varies. The peoples of Oaxaca find fewer general causes in common than the Maya (the authorities are suspected of fomenting division among both). Yet, in 1998, the former succeeded in amending their state constitution with a Law on the Rights of the Indigenous Peoples & Communities.

ECONOMIC OPTIONS

Those who could stay on their own lands maintained much of the ancient knowledge and beliefs, the 'costumbres' and the repertoire of techniques around the hearth and in the field, where a vital condition for preservation was Native language. While, in highland Guatemala, the Indians have long maintained a critical mass of population, their cousins in the mountains north-east of Mexico City and in the south are protected by geographical and economic marginality. A few score Lakandons keep up the pagan life in the dwindling forest of Chiapas, although tourism is now helping to bring them into 'the fold' and the discovery of oil there has led to official interference. As population rose among the mountain Maya, during the mid 1800s, communities retaining enough territory of their own dispersed. Families left the towns to clear new fields or to take advantage of hamlets closer to main roads – hence the 'vacant' municipal centres characteristic of the region today, with many houses only occupied temporarily. In recent decades, similar pressures have drawn them to join the colonization of the forest.

Elsewhere, however, the Indians found themselves surrounded too closely by White and mestizo communities. In Guatemala, despite their own growth, Maya declined by more than 10 per cent as a proportion of total population from 1950 to 1994. The other people needed land too. At Tepoztlán, the proportion of men farming fell from 83 per cent in 1950 to 26 per cent in 1990. In Zincantan, where 90 per cent of male householders grew maize and beans in 1966, only 10 per cent had the land for self-sufficiency by 1980 and, by 1983, 40 per cent had none at all. In another Maya community in the same region, the proportion of land sown in maize and beans fell, in competition with graziers, from 90 per cent in 1950 to 10 per cent in 1990. A.R. Sandstrom has argued that some Nahuas take the relatively expensive option of herding in order to retan claim to unploughed land. A few Huichols, reports Jay Fikes, have resorted to growing cannabis as a cash crop – with dire consequences for everyone's safety.

Not that every change necessarily creates direct conflict. Dr Sandstrom found that, responding to electrification, the people that he studied rearranged their village from a lay-out much like Cerro Gordo (*32*) into a compact grid. Even counting the value of farmland, benefits of 'congregating' may encourage withdrawal even as government squeezes traditional farmers off; but intense use of the remaining land is probably unsustainable and economic disparities widen (*41*); compare the 'Maya collapse' (*25*).

The Indians were not only hemmed in but also pulled out. For, like the Early Colonial haciendas, surrounding communities tried to draw them into work. Trusting their own produce, many mountain Zapotecs obstinately maintain the traditional economy; but, over the past century, more and more Indians did abandon the struggle of subsistence farming. They had three alternatives.

Untold numbers took full-time jobs for wages in towns or on farms and plantations. Most soon adopted the Colonial language and customs. The process had probably started in the sixteenth century. In about 1800, sharp increases of Spanish-speaking mestizos recorded in southernmost Mexico reflected Maya forced off their own lands. Most of the pioneers were men. In the outskirts of Mexico City today, networks have formed to assist indigenous immigrants. During the present generation in Guatemala City, on account of war in the countryside, women have been settling too and new social patterns are developing in shanty suburbs – a type of process familiar in African and Asian cities since 1945. Others fled the fighting to settle on the coast.

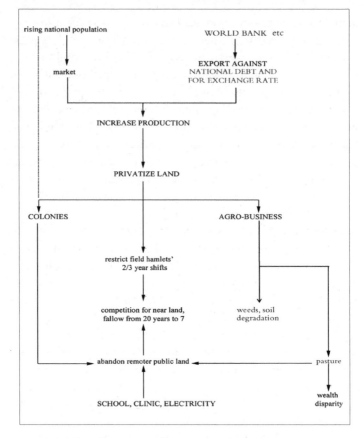

41 North-western Maya willingly abandon remoter land for access to new amenities at the cost of intensifying cultivation while outsiders' demands on that land increase. State policies in capital letters

Second, in order to raise cash for their local civil or ecclesiastical dues, many took up seasonal jobs at plantations. This pattern was especially common among the Maya. Most had to migrate, leaving their folks to cope without them. Not only were working conditions usually bad but also the opportunities were unreliable, depending on national and international prices. In Yucatan, for example, the market for fibre from henequen or sisal (related to maguey) boomed for a century from the 1830s, when much of the country around Mérida was given over to producing it. The mouldering haciendas remain. By the early 1900s began the lumbering, plantations and ranches that have since consumed so much of the forest in the western Maya lowlands. In the 1920s, many thrived in the eastern forests of Yucatan, as in Belize, by collecting 'chicle'; but the market crashed in 1930-1. More recently, the oil fields of the Gulf coast offered opportunities, but that industry slumped in the early 1980s. Many workers then joined the stream of 'wetbacks' to the USA. 1989's collapse of coffee prices had similar effects.

Thirdly, there were opportunities for semi-independent or part-time work. In Oaxaca, traditional life survived the Colonial period comparatively strongly, despite heavy exploitation of labour and energetic production for markets, because the work was done at home and in the local fields and because colonists remained a small minority. During the later 1600s, K'ich'es flourished by cultivating wheat and flocks of sheep. Within a century, however, much of the land exhausted, families in Momostenango took weaving up and started to earn the reputation that they have enjoyed for their textiles to this day. In highland Guatemala and some communities in western Mexico too, 'cottage production' favours household independence (plate 31). However, cheap factory-made wear is weakening demand for traditional woollens.

The cycles of international demand for coffee have had various effects. In the 1890s, as in Guatemala, Maya in Chiapas were dispossessed and taxed off their land in order to make them resort to the new plantations. Fresh demand from the USA, sixty years later, prompted not only plantation but also new roads for carrying the harvest, notably in the mountains of Oaxaca and north of Mexico City. The price in about 1970 encouraged more planting but, by then, the same roads enabled farmers to bring fertilizer for retaining plots of maize on their remaining land. In Chiapas, however, success with other cash crops has varied since use of chemicals proved unsustainable; and some farmers, lacking land at home, have rented plots in the lowlands, either working them seasonally or moving there permanently – the main pressure on the forests.

Some entrepreneurs have responded to new roads by saving and borrowing to buy lorries and coaches – like the muleteers four centuries ago. Construction of the immense beach resort at Cancun, during the 1970s and '80s, created a lot of jobs and many still work there by the week. In the hinterland and elsewhere among the Maya, tourism is stimulating craft production, particularly by women (plate 31). In other parts of Mexico, collectives are producing commodities for sale through the international 'fair trade' movement.

Involvement in the surrounding economy creates wider tensions as well. Enough men still take part to maintain the customary rites; and families returning to their villages at weekends and holidays claim that their jobs are equivalent to traditional tasks, and that to fulfil ceremonial services with cash and the new mass-produced commodities is equivalent to the old 'cargos'; but political fractures are opening.

Novel situations arise too as affluent emigrants faithfully send US dollars back for investment in their villages. In some districts, young men take turns to work in cities in the USA. Emigrants in Mexico City and the USA have set up national and international associations both for local economic and cultural support and to help their people 'back home'.

FIGHTING

Shortage of land for subsistence is the single most critical factor in Native history since the seventeenth century. The symptoms and the consequences are diverse but it has bred strife at three levels.

There were struggles within communities. Where every family needed access to land, the claims of local nobles to control commons grew difficult to sustain and, as they failed, their standing suffered. Kaqchikel lords were locked in litigation with squatters on their private lands in about 1700. The same process was exacerbated among the Mixtecs by soil erosion.

There were conflicts between communities. Sundered from each other by Colonial administration and threatened by the growing populations around them, disputes over boundaries and title became common in most regions. Starting, apparently, in the 1700s, in order to clarify who was using what land, highland Maya communities adopted distinctive hats, shirts and blouses, trousers and skirts (plate 1) – now tourist attractions! Fighting was rife in the mountains of Oaxaca from the 1860s to the 1950s, a vicious circle, since insecurity rendered land unsafe.

Then there were conflicts between Native communities and non-Indians. Most of these confrontations were, and are, with individuals; but, from time to time, they escalated into popular insurrection. Ever since the 1550s, it has been moot as to whether the uprisings are attempts at liberation or (as functionalism predicts – chapter 1) merely 'rebellions', warnings to the authorities about tolerance. That the Maya appear to commemorate them in certain Christian rites and dances shows how difficult it can be to separate armed reactions from spiritual responses. Emboldened by prophecy, Indians in Belize abandoned their approved towns in 1638; but sullen peace did tend to prevail among the Maya during the nadir. Then, violent protests in Tuxtla, in the 1690s, heralded a cycle that is still going on. There was a wave of riots in the Maya highlands in 1701. In 1712, partly in response to repression of folk Catholicism but also to economic concerns, the Holy Virgin was rumoured to have announced that God and the King had died and that the Indians should drive the Spanish out. Colonists' farms and plantations were sacked, the men killed and women and children enslaved. There was a plot to repeat the action in 1847–8 and again in 1868, when war ensued, the Caste War of Chiapas (caste, skin colour). A similar rising happened in Yucatan, in 1761, the leader adopting the name of the last independent lord of Nojpeten, Kanek'. The K'ich'es rioted in protest at the authorities' interference during the last generations of the Colonial period; they armed themselves against encroachers in the 1830s; and they rebelled again in 1876. Not that belligerence is a Maya peculiarity. In Oaxaca, in 1660–1, complaints of extortion led to 10,000 taking up arms. The Huichols rose in 1702 in response to intensified mining and, from the 1850s to the 1890s, joined the Coras and others in an intermittently armed movement for land redistribution. In the 1970s, bitter struggle erupted in Huejutla and, in 1998–9, the southern Zapotecs protested about official molestation.

The Caste War of Yucatan, in 1847–9, was a bid for liberation. It nearly drove all but Indians out. At least a quarter of the population died in direct or indirect consequence of the fighting. The rising

foundered mainly because, economically and politically more bound
to the authorities, the Indians around Mérida refused to join in. Nor
did the highlanders see fit to help. Many of the rebels fled to Belize
(British Honduras), but skirmishes continued into the mid 1850s and
a rump held out – or was ignored – well into the 1900s, maintaining
some of the ancient way of life in the eastern forests.

The 'reconquest' of Guatemala, in 1978-85, killed more than
50,000 Maya and drove nearly a million from home. Thousands
were herded into camps like colonial congregaciones, and trained
in both counter-insurgency and civics. In 1992, the K'ich'e campaigner, Rigoberta Menchú, was awarded the Nobel Peace Prize.

The latest rebellion erupted in 1994, again in the southern
highlands of Mexico. With hindsight, we can see that there were
warnings: between 1970 and 1990, indigenous population had
nearly doubled relative to the rest; the latter had emigrated from
most indigenous districts; and Maya farmers won back some of the
land lost to their ancestors in the Colonial period; but the adjust-
ments were insufficient. On the day that Mexico joined the North
American Free Trade Agreement (NAFTA), San Cristóbal de las
Casas and Ocosingo were occupied by 'Zapatistas' (the EZLN)
in protest against the implications of free trade for subsistence
farming. The rebels persist, in parts of the highlands and amid the
forest, in a political and military confrontation with the authorities
made public, among other means, by deft use of the Internet. The
apparently unmesoamerican Tojolabal experience of coping without exclusive local affiliations was probably an important example
for the movement; and it is telling that the Maya are now joined
by some mestizo farmers. Not all of the Maya are united with
the Zapatistas, partly thanks to government concessions on local
development. The politics are complicated and bitter; the state has
managed to co-opt some traditional leaders. Yet the movement's
vision of regional autonomy and ethnic pluralism is acknowledged
around the world; and it helped to inspire Oaxaca's law on indigenous rights.

Just as the Maya fell foul of the struggle over communism, others
too experienced war of a different kind. The Mexican Revolution
(1910–20) devastated many villages. Mid-twentieth-century anthro-

pologists remarked on suspicion, pessimism and the isolation of families from each other among the Nahuas of Tepoztlán and the long-suffering Zapotecs of Ixtepeji. If the rigours of the 'closed community' were not enough to engender this outlook, surely the Revolution was, when, like many others, both places had to be completely abandoned. In 1932, civil war in El Salvador brought persecution on the Maya, Pipils and others. On the other hand, during the Mexican Revolution, mountain Nahuas contributed troops in return for local concessions.

NEW WORLD

As elsewhere in the Americas and like many other 'Fourth World' peoples, dispossessed and disenfranchised in their own countries, Mesoamericans are finding that their plight no longer seems so lonely. Communities are discovering common cause. In Oaxaca, a growers' union formed in 1989 has stirred political awareness. In 1990-2, the celebrations of Columbus's landing prompted recognition of issues common to all the Native peoples of the Americas.

The Zapatistas have helped to inspire co-operation between political movements as, for instance, in Mexico's Plural National Indigenous Assembly for Autonomy (ANIPA). Indians are also discovering a wider world curious about their way of life, and even that some non-Indians are humble enough to try to listen and learn from them. One remote village discreetly shows sympathetic tourists films about its life and recent fraught history.

Yet there is a paradox. For 400 years, Indians have recognized language as a key to survival. Although names, parts of words, nouns and, later, verbs were affected by the new language, competence in Spanish was unusual before the twentieth century. Then, owing to job opportunities, schooling outside their own villages and better transport, men and youths tended to take it up along with other 'modern' ways, including dress (plate 3); and many communities now speak Spanish only, some deliberately to espouse 'progress'.

There 'may be more options than at any time in the past', remarks R.J. González, or, he warns, 'than ... in the future, since older knowledges may rapidly be lost if ... not transmitted to younger villagers'. Many abandoning their villages and lands failed to 'replicate' the traditional 'model of the world' (chapter 1). In and around the larger towns, more youths are taking pride in their grandparents' languages now; but local schemes for promoting Native language and literacy, including radio programmes, have taken on a big challenge. Mexico's new policy on diversity is very late. Indians may now be able to negotiate more on their own terms but, to the extent that they do assert themselves in the wider world, they will undergo a lot more change.

References and further
reading

The titles recommended here, for readers preferring English, quickly lead to further literature, notably in journals. Most entries for chapter 1 are not repeated for the other chapters.

ABBREVIATIONS
CUP Cambridge: Cambridge University Press
S&M M.E. Smith & M.A. Masson (ed. 2000 *The ancient civilizations of Mesoamerica: a reader* Malden: Blackwell)
SUP Stanford: Stanford University Press
T&H London: Thames & Hudson
UOP Norman: University of Oklahoma Press
UTP Austin: University of Texas Press

CHAPTER I
See first E.R. Wolf (1959 *Sons of the shaking earth* Chicago: University of Chicago Press), including non-Indian history. M.D. Coe & R. Koontz (2008 *Mexico from the Olmecs to the Aztecs* [6th ed.] T&H) and M.D. Coe (2005 *The Maya* [7th ed.] T&H) are complemented by M.E. Miller (2006 *The art of Mesoamerica from the Olmecs to the Aztecs* [4th ed.] T&H), R.E. Blanton et al. (1993 *Ancient Mesoamerica: a comparison of change in three regions* [2nd ed.] CUP) and the ecological approach of W.T. Sanders & B.J. Price (1968 *Mesoamerica: the evolution of a civilization* New York: Random House). On religion prehispanic and since, see D. Carrasco (1990 *Religions of Mesoamerica: cosmovision and ceremonial centers* San Franciso: Harper & Row). For a stimulating analogy with certain Mesoamerican social transformations – including 'a cult of war and human sacrifice' (p.11) – See D. Tuzin (2001 *Social complexity in the making: a case study among the Arapesh of New Guinea* London: Routledge).

    Textbook: S.T. Evans (2008 *Ancient Mexico & Central America: archaeology and culture history* [2nd ed.] T&H). Reference: R. Wauchope and V.R. Bricker (eds

1964-2000 *Handbook of Middle American Indians* [21 volumes] UTP); R.E.W. Adams & M.J. MacLeod (eds 2000 *Mesoamerica* [2 volumes] CUP); D. Carrasco (ed. 2001 *The Oxford encyclopedia of Mesoamerican cultures: the civilizations of Mexico and Central America* [3 volumes] Oxford: Oxford University Press).

Comparison with the Central Andes is fruitful: see F. Katz (1972 *The ancient American civilizations* London: Weidenfeld & Nicolson) and G.W. Conrad & A.A. Demarest (1984 *Religion and empire: the dynamics of Aztec and Inca expansionism* CUP). For wider perspective on Colonial history, see C. Gibson (1966 *Spain in America* New York: Harper & Row).

On whether Nahuatl is from the north, see *American Anthropologist* 103 (2001 p.913). Also cited: B. Tedlock (1992 *Time and the highland Maya* [2nd ed.] p.202 Albuquerque: University of New Mexico Press); E. Durkheim & M. Mauss (ed. R. Needham 1963 *Primitive classification* London: Cohen & West); J. Lockhart (1992 *The Nahuas after the Conquest: a social and cultural history of the Indians of Central Mexico, Sixteenth through Eighteenth centuries* SUP p.15); E.Z. Vogt (1990 *The Zinacantecos of Mexico: a modern Maya way of life* [2nd ed.] Fort Worth: Harcourt Brace Jovanovich p.100); R.S. Carlsen (1997 *The war for the heart and soul of a highland Maya town* UTP p.171); R.E. Blanton et al. (1996 *Current Anthropology* 37 p.1); R. Menchú (ed. E. Burgos-Debray 1984 *I, Rigoberta Menchú, an Indian woman of Guatemala* London: Verso p.20); *Popol Vuh* ed. D. Tedlock (1996 [2nd ed.] New York: Simon & Schuster).

CHAPTER 2

On 'Sweet beginnings' of maize, see *Current Anthropology* 44 (2003 p.675). Figure 9: for the Nahuas, see Sandstrom (cited below for chapter 9) and, for the Maya, B.B. Faust (1998 *Mexican rural development and the plumed serpent: technology and Maya cosmology in the tropical forest of Campeche, Mexico* Westport [Conn.]: Bergin & Garvey). On diet at K'axob, see *Latin American Antiquity* 14 (2003 p.469). Figure 10: the diet was worked out by B.R. Ortiz de Montellano (1990 *Aztec medicine, health and nutrition* New Brunswick: Rutgers Univesity Press), energy in Guatemala by the United Nations Food & Agriculture Organization (ftp://ftp. fao.org/es/esn/nutrition/ncp/guamap.pdf), and the DRIs by the USA National Academy of Sciences Institute of Medicine (http://www.iom.edu/Object.File/ Master/21/372/0.pdf).

CHAPTERS 3-4

The main points are in R.A. Diehl (2004 *The Olmecs, America's first civilization* T&H), J. Marcus & K.V. Flannery (1996 *Zapotec civilization: how urban society evolved in Mexico's Oaxaca Valley* T&H), the little book by R.E. Blanton et al. (1999 *Ancient Oaxaca: the Monte Albán state* CUP), and the big one by W.T. Sanders et al. (1979 *The Basin of Mexico: ecological processes in the evolution of a civilization* New York: Academic).

Also cited: P. Tolstoy in R.J. Sharer & D.C. Grove (eds 1989 *Regional perspectives on the Olmec* CUP); A. Joyce in J.A. Hendon & R.A. Joyce (eds 2004 *Mesoamerican archaeology: theory and practice* Malden: Blackwell); S. Sugiyama (2005 *Human sacrifice, militarism, and rulership: materialization of state ideology at Teotihuacan* CUP); López & López in D. Carrasco et al. (eds 2000 *Mesoamerica's Classic heritage from Teotihuacan to the Aztecs* Boulder: University Press of Colorado); P.

Clastres (1977 *Society against the state* Oxford: Blackwell); E. Pasztory (ed. 1978 *Middle Classic Mesoamerica AD 400-700* New York: Columbia University Press). An article of G.L. Cowgill's is in S&M. For a whiff of the academic anxiety that goes into working out some of what we think we know, see, on the Olmecs, *Antiquity* 81 (2007 p.201).

CHAPTER 5
Start with A. Demarest (2004 *Ancient Maya: the rise and fall of a rainforest civilization* CUP); M.E. Miller (1999 *Maya art and architecture* T&H) is helpful; and note M. León-Portilla (1988 *Time and reality in the thought of the Maya* [2nd ed.] UOP). Reference: R.J. Sharer with L. Traxler (2006 *The ancient Maya* [6th ed.] SUP). Case studies: P.D. Harrison (1999 *The lords of Tikal: rulers of an ancient Maya city* T&H. W.L. Fash (1993 *Scribes, warriors and kings: the city of Copán and the ancient Maya* [2nd ed.] T&H); D.&G. Stuart (2008 *Palenque: eternal city of the Maya* T&H). For news on research projects, see http://www.mesoweb.com; and, on La Milpa, http://www.bu.edu/lamilpa/

    Also cited: P.A. McAnany (1995 *Living with the ancestors: kinship and kingship in ancient Maya society* UTP); O. de Montmollin (1989 *The archaeology of political structure: settlement analysis in a Classic Maya polity* CUP); D. Friedel et al. (1993 *Maya cosmos: 3000 years on the shaman's path* New York: Morrow); J. Marcus (1976 *Emblem and state in the Classic Maya lowlands: an epigraphic approach to territorial organization* Washington: Dumbarton Oaks); for Haviland & Moholy-Nagy, see S&M.

CHAPTER 6
On the Epiclassic and its heritage, see D. Carrasco (2001 *Quetzalcoatl and the irony of empire: myths and prophecies in the Aztec tradition* [2nd ed.] Boulder: University Press of Colorado). For López & López and Pasztory, see the notes for chapter 4; and, on the Maya, those for chapter 5. Also cited: on obsidian at Xochicalco, *Latin American Antiquity* 19 (2008 p.435); D. Webster (2002 *The fall of the ancient Maya: solving the mystery of the Maya collapse* T&H); on diet in Belize, *Latin American Antiquity* 20 (2009, pp. 15, 37); D.N. Jha (1998 *Ancient India in historical outline* [2nd ed.] p.173 New Delhi: Manohar).

CHAPTER 7
The best option to begin with is M.E. Smith (2003 *The Aztecs* [2nd ed.] Malden: Blackwell); and note Diego Durán (1994 [1581] *The history of the Indies of New Spain* (tr. D. Heyden) UOP; the quote is from p.196). On Aztec ideas, see M. León-Portilla (1963 *Aztec thought and culture* UOP; who recites the poem) and I. Clendinnen (1991 *Aztecs: an interpretation* CUP). Nicholson's analysis is in the *Handbook* (cited for chapter 1; Vol. 10). Also cited: E. Brumfiel (1980 *Current Anthropology* 21, 1991 ed. H.R. Harvey *Land and politics in the Valley of Mexico* Albuquerque: University of New Mexico Press), and, for the figurines, in S&M; S.T. Evans (1985 *Journal of Field Archaeology* 12); J. Habermas (1976 *Legitimation crisis* London: Heinemann); and E.D. Purdum & J.A. Paredes (1989 ed. M. Radelet *Facing the death penalty* p.154 Philadelphia: Temple University Press).

CHAPTERS 8-9

C. Gibson (1964 *The Aztecs under Spanish rule: a history of the Indians of the Valley of Mexico, 1519–1810* SUP) is chunky but basic; and complemented by Lockhart (cited for chapter 1). For economic history of both the Aztecs and the Early Colonial period, see the fine study by R. Hassig (1985 *Trade, tribute and transportation: the sixteenth-century political economy of the Valley of Mexico* UOP). For the Maya, see N.M. Farriss (1984 *Maya society under colonial rule: the collective enterprise of survival* Princeton: Princeton University Press) and the short books by R.M. Hill II (1992 *Colonial Cakchiquels: highland Maya adaptation to Spanish rule, 1600-1700* Fort Worth: Harcourt Brace Jovanovich), Vogt (cited for chapter 1) and E.F. Fischer & C. Hendrickson (2003 *Tecpán Guatemala: a modern Maya town in global and local context* Boulder: Westview). On Nahuas, see A.R. Sandstrom (1991 *Corn is our blood: culture and ethnic identity in a contemporary Aztec Indian village* UOP), an excellent book.

Also cited: E.Z. Vogt (1992 *Tortillas for the gods: a symbolic analysis of Zincanteco rituals* (2nd edition UOP); B. Tedlock as for chapter 1 (p.42); L. Nader (1990 *Harmony ideology: justice and control in a Zapotec mountain village* SUP); Wolf as for chapter 1; J.C. Fikes (2004 R.M. Zingg *Huichol mythology* eds J.C. Fikes et al. Tucson: University of Arizona Press p.23); and R.J. González (2001 *Zapotec science: farming and food in the northern sierra of Oaxaca* UTP p.101). Figure 39 is derived from B.B. Faust (cited for chapter 2). 'Compartmentalization' is E.P. Dozier's term (1961 ed. E.H. Spicer *Perspectives in American Indian culture change* Chicago: University of Chicago Press) and 'revitalization', also a concept based on Native North American history, A.F.C. Wallace's (1956 *American Anthropologist* 58).

Index